Gender, Sport and the Role of the Alter Ego in Roller Derby

T0382918

Gender, Sport and the Role of the Alter Ego in Roller Derby focuses on the resurgence of roller derby by examining the appeal and dedication to a sport that combines the masculine aggression and physicality of sport with a more feminine, or alternative, style of organizing and community building.

No longer a scripted sport filled with fake fighting and hair pulling, derby, though still dangerous, has nevertheless exploded in popularity around the world. Drawing on data from in-depth interviews with women players, Colleen Arendt reveals how derby has come to serve as a site of gender rebellion and emancipation that empowers participants. She demonstrates how players find roller derby a place to build friendships and support networks, while giving back to their community. The book also analyzes the adoption of derby personas, or alter egos, which many players use. While many players derive joy and other benefits from their derby personas, others argue that personas and alter egos detract from the athleticism and legitimacy of the sport. Finally, by considering the relationship between gender, sport, society, and power, this book tries to answer the question: Why derby? Why now?

Colleen E. Arendt is an Associate Professor in the Department of Communication Studies at Concordia University, St. Paul, United States. Her research interests lie at the intersection of organizational communication, gender, feminisms, and sport. She often focuses her research on gendered careers, such as the military, nursing, and STEM.

Gender, Sport and the Role of the Alter Ego in Roller Derby

Colleen E. Arendt

Routledge
Taylor & Francis Group

LONDON AND NEW YORK

First published 2019 by Routledge

2 Park Square, Milton Park, Abingdon, Oxfordshire OX14 4RN

52 Vanderbilt Avenue, New York, NY 10017

Routledge is an imprint of the Taylor & Francis Group, an informa business

First issued in paperback 2020

British Library Cataloguing-in-Publication Data
A catalogue record for this book is available from the British Library

Library of Congress Cataloging-in-Publication Data
Names: Arendt, Colleen E., author.
Title: Gender, sport and the role of the alter ego in roller derby / Colleen E. Arendt.
Description: Abingdon, Oxon ; New York, NY : Routledge, 2019. | Includes bibliographical references and index.
Identifiers: LCCN 2018018359 | ISBN 9781138569102 (hardback : alk. paper) | ISBN 9780203704400 (ebook)
Subjects: LCSH: Roller derby—Social aspects. | Roller derby—Physiological aspects. | Women roller skaters—Psychology. | Ego (Psychology)
Classification: LCC GV859.6 .A74 2019 | DDC 796.21—dc23
LC record available at https://lccn.loc.gov/2018018359

ISBN: 978-1-138-56910-2 (hbk)
ISBN: 978-0-367-49236-6 (pbk)

Typeset in Times New Roman
by Apex CoVantage, LLC

To my daughters, Madeline and Natalie. I love you.

Contents

Acknowledgments

This book would not be possible were it not for the amazing women who participated in my study. I am forever grateful for your time, trust, and insights. I want to thank my family for the endless hours you watched the girls so I could write. I could not have finished this book without you. Thank you to Dr Patrice Buzzanell for being the (brilliant) embodiment of a feminist mentor, leader, and friend. I could never pay you back, so I'll try to pay it forward. Thank you also to Dr Emily Orlando and Dr Johanna Garvey for being amazing colleagues and mentors. Finally, thank you to my colleague and friend, Dr Audra Nuru, for your encouragement and support of this endeavor, and for your invaluable feedback.

1 Introduction

The resurgence of roller derby

With origins dating back to the 1920s, roller derby has seen a resurgence in the past few years. A Hollywood movie, *Whip It*, books, social media, and even televised games have renewed interest in the sport. Roller derby is a contact sport combining physicality with strategy as well as a strong sense of community among teams and leagues. The resurgence of flat track roller derby began in 2001 in Austin, Texas with the Texas Roller Girls and has grown to more than 450 leagues worldwide, in part due to the relatively small capital needed to begin a league (WFTDA, 2016). This contributes to the do-it-yourself grassroots appeal of the sport that allows leagues to tailor themselves to their community and the women who participate.

The women who compete in roller derby leagues all over the world are dedicated to this physically demanding sport while juggling the demands of their lives, including families and "mainstream" careers like teaching, finance, and law. Roller derby is often considered to be the most violent of women's sports, borrowing the term "bouts" for their matches because they are "a fight to the end" (WFTDA, 2016). Many events require EMTs on site and online forums are dedicated to discussing injuries.

Based on nearly 3,000 minutes of data collected across forty in-depth interviews with women players, this book focuses on the draw and dedication to a sport that combines the masculine aggression and physicality of sport with a more feminine, or alternative, style of organizing and community building. In the early years of its revival, derby contained more overt sexuality, seen through their outfits (some women wore tutus and fishnet stockings), logos, and promotional photographs and apparel, that is usually absent from men's athletic contests. As the sport has grown in popularity around the world, some cultural aspects of the sport, including the counterculture, kitsch, theatricality, and sexuality, has disappeared as streamlined rules and uniforms emerged and participants' athleticism and skill level increased.

This book examines various aspects of roller derby through five chapters, followed by the methodology of my study in the Appendix.

- Chapter 1 introduces the sport, with a brief primer on the rules, positions, and leagues. This chapter also discusses misperceptions of roller derby, including (a) the misconception that derby is merely staged fighting, complete with hair pulling and throwing elbows and (b) the misconception of derby as filled with hypersexualized, dangerous women.
- Chapter 2 examines obstacles the women face in their quest to play the sport, including the large time and financial commitment, and the promise of serious injuries.
- Chapter 3 follows by examining why the women continue to play – and love – a sport despite the serious challenges detailed in Chapter 2.
- Chapter 4 discusses what many outsiders consider the most interesting aspect of the sport: the derby personas, or the pseudonyms the women play under. When roller derby reemerged in 2001, alter egos, or separate selves, dominated the landscape of the game. Now that the game is growing and evolving, the alter egos are largely disappearing in favor of derby personas, which are less extreme personality differences the women experience by skating under inventive, clever pseudonyms they create.
- Chapter 5 attempts to answer the overarching question of my study: *Why derby? Why now?* What is it about the sport that has helped it grow and thrive – even during the financial collapse of 2008 – when its athletes report large expenses, a time commitment that is akin to a part-time job, and numerous serious injuries (e.g., broken bones, torn ligaments, reparative surgeries)? Not only do the women remain in the sport, but everyone I spoke with discussed plans to remain involved in derby in some fashion after retiring from competition. Chapter 5 connects my findings to existing literatures in my attempt to answer the question: *Why derby? Why now?* Chapter 5 additionally explores societal constraints and moments of social emancipation and activism, befitting the critical theory lens employed in this study.
- Finally, the Appendix provides the methodology of the book, including information on qualitative methodology, ontological framework, participants, procedures, and data analysis.

Following this brief synopsis of the book, I return now to an overview of the sport.

A gendered perspective

Throughout this study, I examined my data through a gendered perspective, specifically one that considers gender as a social construct. Gender as socially constructed refers to gender as "an emergent feature of social situations: both as an outcome of and a rationale for various social arrangements, and as a means of legitimating one of the most fundamental divisions of society" (West & Zimmerman, 2002, p. 4). Moreover, gender is what defines our "roles, rights, and responsibilities and obligations" (Vasiljević, Marling, & Örtenblad, 2017, p. 4). In other words, gender has been "nurtured" into us by socially constructed institutions that serve to divide the sexes.

The process through which individuals learn these "gender norms" is known as gender socialization. Because gender is a "historical phenomenon" (Alvesson & Billing, 2009, p. 9), gender norms change across time and within and between cultures. Thus, as Wharton (2012) says, to study gender is to take "an interest in a moving target" (p. 103). By studying roller derby at this point in its revival and against the larger backdrop of the current social, economic, and political landscape in the United States means that I seek to understand the ways roller derby and gender inform each other.

While gender norms socialize people to enact differing gender roles, crucially, these roles confer different social statuses. Vasiljević et al. (2017) explain, "Gender difference is also a hierarchy in which practices and behaviors associated with men have historically been valued higher than those linked to women, resulting in women's disadvantaged status in all spheres of society" (p. 4). Thus, to "see" gender roles and norms, and the power structures inherent in the gendered socialization of men and women, is to call attention to the inequalities and inequities entrenched in a gendered society, and to search for opportunities to subvert this domination.

The sport of roller derby

Rules and positions

Modern day roller derby is played on a flat, oval track. Two teams compete in two, 30-minute halves. Each half is filled with jams that last up to two minutes. During each jam, both teams field five skaters. Of the five skaters, four are blockers, and the fifth skater for each team is the "jammer," denoted by wearing a helmet cover with a large star. Each team's jammer starts the jam behind the eight blockers. The two jammers need to fight through the pack of blockers. After that initial passing of the blockers, a jammers then circles around and earns a point for each opposing player she passes. In other words, the jammer fights through the pack at the beginning of the jam and then circles around and passes everyone on the opposing team, earning five points. The blockers, meanwhile, are simultaneously trying to block the other team's jammer while creating opportunities for their own jammer to break through the pack.

At the beginning of a jam, when the two jammers start behind the eight blockers, the jammer who breaks through the pack first is called the "lead jammer." This means she can end the jam at any point, which is why a jam can be "up to two minutes long." Typically, a lead jammer, e.g., *Jammer 1*, might call a jam just before the other jammer, e.g., *Jammer 2*, is about to score points. That means Jammer 2 needs to fight through the pack and place herself in scoring position as quickly as possible, because even if the jam is called before she can score, she also held Jammer 1 to few points. Because the oval track is not very large, allowing numerous laps, and because the 60 minutes of competition is comprised of many jams, teams often score in the 100s and 200s.

Though derby is a contact sport, rules prohibit many types of contact. Despite misconceptions, skaters cannot throw elbows, push, pull, or trip opponents, and they cannot block from behind. Rules also prohibit making contact to opponents' heads, back, knees, lower legs, or feet (WFTDA, 2018). Skaters typically make contact with opponents by bumping each other, which is why one of my participants referred to the sport as a "collision" sport rather than a contact sport. Skaters have more flexibility in how they make contact with their own teammates. A jammer can use an "arm whip," which occurs when a blocker extends her arm to her jammer and then propels the jammer forward as a transfer of momentum, or a "hip whip," which is similar but refers to a jammer grabbing one of her blocker's hips and pulling herself forward.

Because the athletes are moving quickly on skates, the collisions and tripping or tangling of skates can lead to serious injuries, as I discuss in Chapter 2. Injuries can also occur from illegal hits, which are penalized by the skater sitting in the penalty box for 30 seconds of the jam, leaving their team to play shorthanded. If a jammer is sent to the penalty box, the thirty-second penalty is referred to as a "power jam," as only one team can score points. Sometimes a lead jammer will call a jam when the other team's jammer heads to the penalty box so they can start a fresh jam, perhaps with a new, rested jammer, to maximize scoring opportunities for those 30 seconds the other team is without their jammer.

Another important element of the game is the pivot. Each team can designate one of the four blockers as their pivot, denoted by wearing a helmet cover with a large stripe on it. At any point during a jam, a jammer can take off her star helmet cover and hand it to the pivot, who then puts on the star helmet cover and is now the jammer and can score points. The star helmet cover must be handed; it cannot be thrown or picked up by the pivot. The previous jammer is now a blocker and is no longer able to score points for the duration of that jam.

"Stars in my eyes"

I asked participants what position of the three – jammer, blocker, pivot – they usually play, or prefer to play, and why. Brooke knew she wanted to jam the first time she saw a bout: "I was like, 'That's what I want to be.' And a friend of mine said she saw stars in my eyes when I was watching it." When I asked her specifically what it is about jamming that appeals to her, she said: "It's just the feeling I get when I get through the pack . . . chasing down the girl in front of me. I really like that." Brooke sees the pack of blockers as a puzzle:

> So you come up to [the pack] and you've got all these girls, and four of them have this fire like they're trying to kill you and four of them are trying to help you and you have to read what all of them are doing, so it's like you've got this sort of puzzle in front of you and it's constantly changing and you constantly have to adjust.

Eliza also likes being the jammer, because even though getting through the pack is a complicated proposition, she feels more of a singular purpose: "I feel like I have a more singular purpose and I actually can focus on it better." In contrast, blocking requires multitasking, a weakness for her: "It's just hard for me to multitask . . . it's just there are like eight or nine things that I need to keep track of when I'm a blocker (laughs), and my mind is overwhelmed at times." Jordan finds it challenging and a bit lonely: "[Jamming is] stressful also but I like the challenge. I find it lonely sometimes." Maura understands the loneliness of jamming but enjoys when all five skaters are "in sync":

> I think a lot of people miss sort of the teamwork aspect of jamming, because a lot of people think that you're on your own and you just kind of do your thing. But having a relationship with your pack where you're leading what they're hopefully doing for you, I think once that gets in sync, it's really kind of a weird, mental, cool relationship.

"The action in the pack"

Rae understands why people love jamming, but she prefers the "action in the pack" as a blocker: "I feel like when everybody starts they want to be a jammer because the glory is in the jammer because she's the one who's scoring all the points, but I like the action in the pack." Ruth sees the importance of blockers to the game: "I think jammers have a messiah complex that's not a good thing because you feel like I can take care of everything myself . . . [but] a jammer's only as good as the other four people out there skating with her."

Some of the women prefer to block because of their size. While Eliza likes to jam because she is smaller than many and cites speed and agility as two of her strengths, Tina likes to block even though she is "5'2 and weighs about 100 pounds." She explained her strategy: "Rather than me being able to lay big girls OUT I can just get in front of them and sit on them and block them that way. So you just use what you have."

It was no surprise to me that Natalie loves blocking as her derby name refers to blocking. She explained the appeal of blocking: "It makes me feel really powerful to be like, 'You're not going to get past me and you're not going to score.' It's my decision, like 'I'm better than you. I can stop you.'"

Only two women mentioned the pivot position. One merely lumped pivot and blocker together, while Ruth had this to say about the pivot: "Pivot is a very difficult position that might not get as much recognition as jamming . . . if pivots are doing their jobs they're calling shots and telling people where they should be." Ruth does not like pivot because knowing teammate's strengths and then directing them is not a strength of hers:

> I'm not so strong of a pivot. I don't want to tell someone to hold the inside line or help the jammer through if I can't be confident they can do that. There's some people who have no problem asking that of strangers and that's a good quality.

"Chess on roller skates"

Many women, like Ruth, described the complexity of the game and cited it as a reason they love the sport. Rae used a metaphor common to my participants to describe derby – chess on skates: "You're playing both offense and defense at the same time, like a fast-paced chess game on roller skates. You have to be really quick on your feet."

The chess aspect Rae is referring to is the fact that blockers have to simultaneously block one jammer while creating openings for, or sometimes coming to aid of, their own jammer. This is different from other sports. Though people might compare derby to basketball or soccer because of the offense and defense aspect, whether a player is playing offense or defense at any given moment is determined by who has the ball. In derby, skaters play both simultaneously. Even as a blocker might act offensively in one second to help her jammer, she must remain mindful of how a particular movement will impact the opposing jammer.

Hearing their soul when you hit them

Along with the strategy aspect of derby, another reason women cited loving the sport is the contact nature of derby – or rather, "getting to hit people." When discussing this project with people unaffiliated with derby, I am always surprised by people who do not think women would enjoy a contact sport the way it is taken for granted that men do. Many of the women laughed or qualified their statement saying they know it sounds bad, but they like hitting people in derby. Rae said: "It's really exciting and I like to hit people. There's that too (laughs)." Audra also laughed and qualified the following statement, acknowledging how "messed up" it is to say: "I mean, I know (laughs) maybe this sounds messed up to say but my favorite part of derby is getting to hit people. You know, knock the crap out of people (laughs) so I'm definitely drawn to that." Julie prefers to hit rather than be hit, because a jammer who hits is wasting her energy. Therefore, she prefers blocking to jamming: "Yeah, I mean I like to hit people. Ya know, it's much more easy to hit people when you are the blocker cause if you're the jammer hitting people, you're getting rid of a lot of energy." Natalie describes her pleasure in making contact as a bit shallow: "On a shallow level, just hearing people when you hit them, just slowly letting their soul out. It feels very empowering."

League design and tryouts

I now provide background into how leagues are established as well has how some leagues run tryouts. My intention in providing this background is to underscore that derby is a legitimate sport with rules, procedures, and a competitive selection process. The way individual leagues are designed depends on their initial size, how quickly they are able to grow, and the skill level and athleticism of its players. For example, when a new league forms, if they wish to join the Women's Flat Track Derby Association, they need to be sponsored by an existing league. Once sponsored, they become an apprentice league, which usually lasts one year.

Leagues often choose to divide the women into a handful of teams, frequently referred to as *home teams*, and these teams bout publicly every few weeks in a round-robin format. Imagine a public intramural league that charges admission. Teams use the money earned from admissions and any merchandise to support their league, including rental space for their practice and bout locations. Some reported bouting in small venues in front of tiny crowds, while other women report playing in front of 5,000+ people in venues that they change every year as they increasingly need larger venues. Some women play in leagues that are televised on cable access channels.

In addition to home teams, a WFTDA-affiliated league will create a travelling team. The travel team is typically composed of the best players from each home team. The traveling team competes against other leagues either a few hours' drive away or across the country, or even internationally. The traveling bouts are what the WFTDA use to calculate world rankings. The profits from bouts also go toward deferring the costs of travel for these skaters. The best skaters do not always comprise the travel teams; some women opt to play only for their home team because they are unable to meet the extra commitments involved in being on the traveling team. In contrast, some leagues have moved toward a policy of letting those skaters on traveling teams quit their home teams. This might free up 5–6 hours of practice each week, but as Natalie explained, a major drawback is a skater loses her local fan base:

> The biggest change I made was I quit the home team this year. And that's kind of a big deal . . . You give up a lot of cool things about derby to not be on a home team. You give up being the best player on your team cause you're an all-star player and you give up those fans that follow you.

Maura explained how rosters for traveling teams work:

> The way it works for a top team that's registered to play in WFTDA is they have a charter that is composed of 20 skaters . . . But the number of people who actually play in a bout are 14, and there are two alternates that get named in case something happens to one of the other 14 girls, then they get to play. So you essentially have six skaters that will not be playing off of this charter, and coming onto [the roster] typically means you're at the bottom and you're one of these six skaters that's stuck in this limbo of whether or not you'll actually get to play.

A number of participants, particularly those who created their league or who branched off and formed a new one, are pleased when their leagues grows to the extent that they can form A, B, and C traveling teams, though only the A team's record counts toward their ranking.

That type of growth can take time. Some of the new leagues might not have enough athletes to fill more than two home teams their first year. Kate detailed a mistake her team made when they initially formed. They divided the forty skaters they had their first year into two teams of twenty and they would bout each other a few times a year. She explained what this design did for team unity:

> That was a horrible, horrible setup, because when you have two home teams you bout every time. It wasn't good for team unity. It sort of

divided the team as you can imagine. It wasn't good for sharing information and teaching and learning.

After two years in that format, they moved to two traveling teams: "an A and B team, who would play other leagues' A and B teams."

Then there is Madeline's league, which is such an elite league that, at least for a few years, their traveling A team could not play other A teams located relatively nearby, so they would send their B or C traveling team in their place. Meanwhile their elite traveling A team has to travel cross country – and even internationally – to compete against teams of the same caliber. Madeline explained that the traveling A team tries to be "pretty selective" in who they bout:

> They want someone that's the same caliber, and not just "Sure, we'll play your tiny team's traveling team." Cause then the score would come out to be something like four to five hundred to almost nothing. It would almost be a complete embarrassment like "Yea, you really want to send your amateur team to our pro level team." (laughs)

While her words may sound harsh, in reality, this design remains one way for area leagues to improve, as well as her own elite league to develop all their athletes. For a sport that has taken off around the country and world at various junctures, some of the earlier leagues, especially the ones in more populated areas who draw from a larger pool of athletes, simply dominate until others catch up.

The way leagues organize tryouts varies by how much interest there is (how many women show up), how new the league is, and how skilled the athletes are. A few of the women I spoke with created their leagues, and when they began, they did not have traditional tryouts where some athletes are cut. Instead, women had to learn and then pass a series of skills tests before they could bout. Julie, who branched off from an existing league to help create a new one in the same city, explained how her league has easy tryouts compared to that older, more-established league:

> I know that [the other local team] goes through a pretty rigorous tryout process, whereas we just have an intake workshop where we just run people through all the paces and show them what they can expect, and then if they want to sit around, then they're a member of the league.

On the other extreme are the more competitive, veteran leagues. One skater, Natalie, who plays for one of the best teams in the world, described 130 skaters trying out for 2–3 openings in a once-a-year tryout that lasted two months:

> I showed up and there are 130 girls. I don't know if they're good or bad or their backgrounds or whatnot. And I know in my head that there are three spots, so I kind of freaked out like "What am I doing?" (laughs) It's a two-month tryout. It's not just one night, it's two months of them watching you and whittling down people every week. It's very, very nerve-wracking. (laughs)

While this was one example of an elite, internationally ranked team, as the sport grows in both popularity and athleticism, skaters could expect to see similarly competitive tryouts. For women like Julie who have played in large leagues and brand-new leagues (which she happened to help found), figuring out a way to meet the needs of the various skaters on home teams and/or traveling teams can be a daunting proposition. She described seeing her new league grow: "I think for us, because we've had such exponential growth, it's been really difficult to manage that. You know, we started as a group of ten people, and now we have, I think, 60 skaters." She explained that while they are now a member of the WFTDA, meaning they can be ranked internationally, she does not want to forget about other skaters: "I also wanted to make sure we maintain a focus on all those skaters that don't get to skate at the top-tier level . . . We need to govern ourselves in a way that meets everyone's needs."

"Sport versus spectacle": fighting misperceptions and negative portrayals

Learning of the "exponential growth" of Julie's league did not surprise me, given that the sport has seen incredible growth around the world in fewer than two decades. Yet many players still deal with a common misconception of modern day roller derby: that derby is fake, or scripted. In other words, when many people hear about roller derby today, their minds flash back to the days of fake fighting, including elbow throwing and hair pulling. Though participants admit they enjoy the rough, dangerous contact element of the sport, they want to disabuse people that the sport is not in any way connected to earlier, decades-old versions of derby that included fake fighting along the lines of WWE/WWF wrestling. Sophia described this evolution:

> It was big in the 70s. It's a little bit different now, it's not quite what it used to be. It used to be more kind of just you got tricks and things, and

it was like WWF wrestling where you throw elbows and you pull girls' hair and you start fights and you trip, and it was kind of ridiculous. And it died out I guess for a while, and then in the early 2000s there was a league in Texas that kind of picked it back up again (laughs). And so anyways, it's grown quite a bit.

Brooke said she just has to "roll her eyes" when she hears people with misperceptions of derby as straight brutality:

> The perception of roller derby is quite different from what the actuality of it is . . . I think that most people think that roller girls are just out to hurt each other . . . But it's like (laughs) a lot more than that . . . not just straight brutality. (laughs)

Patrice also deals with the misperceptions: "So much of the stigma around roller derby is what it was in the 70s when it was televised and a lot of it was dramatized, created stage wrestling for entertainment purposes." Instead of rolling her eyes, Patrice tries to break the "stigma" around the sport:

> There's so many people that think that's what derby is. To be able to break that stigma and really show that it's a full contact sport for woman and that they're really athletes and that it's an amazing thing to watch. It's just wonderful.

"Who wants their kid to turn out like that?"

Another misperception of derby is that derby women are hypersexualized. Jordan explained:

> When we first started it was really like (pause) image focused, like people wanted to be in derby because they wanted to be in a CALENDAR or on roller skates and look sexy and all of that. I think that element is still there but it's really moved to being a really competitive sport, focused environment as well.

Julie also compared derby today to just a few years ago when she began watching bouts:

> It's kind of crazy cause I first got into it 'cause it was just so punk rock and DIY and people were wearing crazy things and the DJ was spinning underground music. It's definitely slowly gotten to [be] more

athletic where people are wearing actual clothes that make sense to roller skate in.

Julie remembers the first time she saw derby since its resurgence and the skaters were wearing corsets: "The very first season one of the teams, they skated in corsets. I cannot even fathom somebody skating in something that can actually constrict your breathing while you are trying to do this (laughs)."

Additionally, many of the women shared their frustration with outsiders' focus on their derby persona, or alter ego, as being a "librarian by day and a sexy derby girl by night." According to Emma: "People come out and want to interview us all the time, but yeah, it is kind of like the same story, and each journalist thinks . . . 'I really have this great angle,' and it's like, 'We've read this story a thousand times that you just wrote' (laughs)."

In addition to being hypersexualized, derby women are often portrayed as dangerous women. Lynn discussed negative television portrayals on shows like *CSI: New York* and *Hawaii Five-0*: "I don't think derby has a great image on TV. It is all about how these girls are killers and they're mean, and that's just not at all what roller derby's about." She raised an interesting point about the impact of these portrayals on the development of the sport: "I think we're going to be meeting resistance to starting a junior league, because who wants to their kid to turn out like that? Nobody. But we're not – none of the leagues I know are really like that at all." Lynn, who is living and playing in a depressed rural town nevertheless thinks her brand-new – and small – league needs to eventually expand to include a junior league:

> I'd love to do something like junior derby eventually, get the kids exercising because we have a huge obesity problem and problems with diabetes and just health in general. Because, you know, we're in a depressed rural town. But I don't think we're going to be able to do that until we get some [positive] exposure and show them what derby is actually about.

Similarly, Lucy told me that she tries to record and watch every instance of roller derby's portrayal on televisions shows. She likewise noticed a pattern:

> One of the things that I think is really funny and I noticed it in a lot of the portrayals have been that there's always a lot of resistance to outsiders and even when people are cooperating they're still very skeptical. I get that if the police officer were coming up to my roller derby league and was sitting asking questions about something, I would maybe be very cautious but I would certainly be cooperative.

Lucy adds that in many portrayals, a character has to go undercover to "infiltrate" a league. She finds that funny because when it comes to tryouts: "We welcome those people. We try to embrace them and get to know them . . . In general our philosophy in my league is if someone's coming to us and they're trying to join us, we get to know them, be welcoming . . . It's a global kind of community. But in all of these shows, they're very resistant to the new people they're inviting in." She concluded: "That's not how I experience roller derby."

This chapter introduced roller derby as a sport by discussing its resurgence, rules, positions, and league design, including how some leagues organize tryouts. This chapter also illustrated misperceptions and negative portrayals skaters have to counter with various publics. The next chapter analyzes major challenges women face in their quest to play and remain in the sport: steep financial and time commitments, and the prospect of serious injury.

References

Alvesson, M. & Billing, Y.D. (2009). *Understanding gender and organizations* (2nd ed.). Los Angeles, CA: Sage.

West, C. & Zimmerman, D.H. (2002). Doing gender. In *Doing Gender, doing difference: Inequality, power, and institutional change* (pp. 3–25). New York, NY: Routledge.

Wharton, A.S. (2012). *The sociology of gender: An introduction to theory and research* (2nd ed.). West Sussex, UK: Wiley–Blackwell.

Women's Flat Track Derby Association [WFTDA]. (2016). Frequently asked questions. Retrieved from: https://wftda.org/faq

Women's Flat Track Derby Association [WFTDA]. (2018). The rules of flat track roller derby. Retrieved from: https://rules.wftda.com/

Vasiljević, S., Marling, R., & Örtenblad, A. (2017). Introduction: Different dimensions of gender equality in a comparative perspective. In A. Örtenblad, R. Marling, & S. Vasiljević (Eds.), *Gender equality in a global perspective* (pp. 3–19). New York, NY: Routledge.

2 Obstacles to playing roller derby

While the previous chapter outlined the resurgence of roller derby and discussed a few of the ways leagues are organized around the country, this chapter discusses what perhaps surprised me most from the interviews: the many reasons that might prevent a woman from playing roller derby. This chapter examines three main obstacles to playing: (a) the expensive nature of the sport, (b) the rigorous time commitments, and (c) the very common, often *very* serious injuries players suffer. To outsiders, derby being a "hobby" that is akin to a part-time job, that you have to pay significant expenses in order to participate in, all while under the constant threat of incurring a serious injury, might seem like three reasonable reasons for avoiding or quitting roller derby. However, for the participants, these hurdles do not prevent them from playing.

Financial commitment

When I asked about any negatives that come from playing roller derby, most women invariably mentioned two things: the cost and the time commitment. Participating can be very expensive because of dues, uniforms and other equipment, and travel expenses for those who play on traveling teams (some leagues do reimburse some travel expenses; for example, for their all-star or their traveling teams). A quick Google search of "Roller derby starter kits" shows a range of equipment packages, mostly ranging from $250–600, for skates, helmet, mouth guard, elbow and knee pads, and wrist guards.

Sarah said that expenses are not just for her individual uniform and equipment needs:

> We pay for our dues, we pay for our uniforms. We pay for anything. We donate things to the Warehouse because like we need new cones so we can practice with cones. You know someone will be like, "OK I'll donate some cones." WE donate everything.

Bridgett used a calculator during the interview to calculate her expenses. She figures she pays $240/year in dues, $60 in insurance – as the women are required to have insurance through the leagues – and approximately $300 in equipment, not counting the nearly $600 she had just put toward new skates, which she notes should last her for years. She adds:

> There's probably things I'm forgetting too, like, if you want to include things like gas, I mean, you could include gas. I have to go to practice, like, three days a week, so you could do that. And there's also, like, travel expenses to away bouts.

Brooke mentioned the relief she felt when her mom bought her an expensive pair of skates:

> When she offered for my dad and her to buy me a new pair of skates, I was like (gasp). You know, it saved my life, because I don't know how long it would have taken me to get the hundreds of dollars that it cost me to get a really good quality pair.

Suzy mentioned that in just travel costs, she probably spends "a couple thousand dollars a year traveling."

Many of the women discussed the impact the financial commitment has on their ability and willingness to continue playing. Maura, a graduate student living off loans, said: "Also financially, I'm – I don't have a job, I live off the student loans, and it's pretty hard to keep up the equipment requirements." Lucy said that what would keep her from derby is not injuries, because "physically, I'm doing okay." However, for her, the "limitation is more or less financial because the cost of driving to everything all the time. I did the math and it got really discouraging. Not to mention that we pay dues every month for the privilege of skating." She continued:

> That is the thing that I see as the biggest threat to me continuing but at this point. It's something that I'm able to manage and willing to make sacrifices and maybe it's not the most wise financial choice, but I'm in a position where it's not a danger.

Sophia also seems to have been conducting a cost-benefit analysis of playing following an injury that required surgery: Sophia said:

> When I . . . had that [ankle fracture] surgery and I was out of work for a week, it kind of made me think twice about, maybe derby is wonderful and means a lot to me, but at the same time, it doesn't pay the bills.

In summary, while the women love playing derby, as Lucy said, financially speaking, "It can be a little bit foolish."

Time commitment

Not only does roller derby not pay the bills, and women have to pay for everything, they are also required to devote a tremendous amount of time each week to their league. In a country that is overworked and underpaid (Wilkie, 2017), the time commitment alone would be enough to scare many away.

I asked all the women how much time they estimate they spend on roller derby – and the numbers shocked me. Many said they spend over twenty hours per week on roller derby, from practices and extra conditioning, travel time, to their committee work. Madeline likened it to a part-time job: "I would say, it's a part time job. Almost 20 hours a week." Rae sees it as a full-time job that she takes "very seriously":

> It would be over 40 hours a week that I commit to derby. It's a full-time job for me and I take it very seriously. I know we don't get paid to do it, we actually pay to play, but I've been doing it for 7 years now and it's become such a big part of my life . . . It's 40 to 60 hours a week usually.

When I asked Eliza to estimate how much time she devotes to derby, she responded: "Okay, maybe it's easier to gather my free time. Yeah, because it's (laughs) kind of crazy." She noted that they have to do "extra credit," which for her league refers to outside fitness or attending open skating. She continued: "I could probably easily say like twenty-five hours a week that I devote to derby. Probably closer to thirty. Let me mull that over, but I'd say probably thirty is probably accurate."

League requirements

The reason the women spend so much time per week is due to the league requirements. Others in addition to Eliza mentioned the extra credit requirement as well. Andrea explained the minimum practice requirement each player needs to meet:

> I'm constantly looking at my calendar to say, "Okay, there are ten practices this month. In order for me to get my 60%, which is the minimum, here are the practices I have to go to, and here is the extra-credit I have to go to, and here are the events . . ." For me, because I do have a family

and a full-time job, I have to always be sure that I'm conscious that I'm meeting my requirements.

The stakes for meeting the requirements are high. She added: "If you don't make practice, you don't bout the next month."

In addition to their practices – either with the team or their own conditioning – and travel time to those practices, the women devote copious time to their committee work. All the women mentioned that they have to participate on at least one committee. Lucy said she tries to prepare women for the intense time commitment during the tryout period:

> It's not your pick-up basketball game. It's not your once a week for an hour soccer scrimmage. It's more than that. Besides the physical practicing and those elements of the training both in and outside, there's making the business run. Everyone has a responsibility. Even the minimum is a little bit demanding.

Unfortunately, despite warning the "fresh meat," as rookies are called, she noted, "there are always people who – it doesn't register, doesn't click, and then it becomes reality and they can't make the commitment or they don't want to make the commitment, or their priorities change." Rae also discussed explaining to outsiders why derby takes up so much time:

> I tell people we pay to play, but as far as where I'm at, it's like being on a professional team because . . . we do all the grunt work. We run the business . . . We're our managers and we're our PR people. We do everything.

What Rae means by grunt work is that the various committees include responsibilities like setting up and taking down the track. Many women do not bout in their practice facilities, so they have to physically take down and set up the track.

Other committees include marketing and public relations, or NERDS, *New Recruitment and Development*. Sarah described NERDS as: "We do evaluation for new girls who were trying to move up through the ranks and we give them feedback to say yes you're doing well and you're moving up to the new stage or you need to work on these new skills." Others have to do data entry, such as logging everyone's attendance requirements, or the money they make from bouts. Many women mentioned charity work, such as Sarah who said "We have an entire charity committee. Once a month we also go out into the community for charity." Some of the leagues have a charity they donate some of their proceeds from bouts to, which again requires a committee to scout and select various charities. As a result of steep, though often rewarding, league requirements, skaters must navigate finding balance in their lives.

Finding balance?

Between the practices, commuting, and committee work, combined with the responsibilities to their families and their jobs, I asked participants: *How do you balance it all?* I received a variety of responses, some humorous. Nearly everyone found the question itself humorous. Maura responded,

> Oh, not well (laughs). Because I am in the doctoral program, it's extremely competitive and busy, and I have to use a large calendar-like system and keep track of everything I absolutely have to get done by certain days.

Ruth agreed that she also does not do a good job of balancing everything but her supportive spouse helps: "Probably not very well actually, but I have the benefit of having a very supportive spouse . . . my practice was a priority for him also. So he would encourage me to let roller derby be a priority in my life." She added that she stretched her five-year doctoral program to seven years:

> I had a kid and played roller derby so I did a 7-year PhD. Probably, I joke that one year was having my daughter and one year was the 3 years I played roller derby. There was time because I would work hard every day on the tasks before me, but just wearing a lot of hats.

Emma had perhaps the funniest answer to the question of how they find balance when she responded: "I underachieve at work (laughs). It's funny, but it's true, so that I can put that kind of effort and time into the sport."

Another method of "finding balance" is to go without sleep. Many of the women mentioned a lack of sleep. Alexis said:

> Everything is kind of just on an as-needed basis and pretty much I'm just trying to make sure I get enough sleep . . . I have to commute an hour for work so many times I have to drive straight from work to practice and sleep in my car for an hour (laughs) and stuff like that so I don't know if balance is the word I would use. (laughs)

She mentioned having to pull over halfway and take a nap before conducting our interview or that she usually will take a nap at lunch but added:

"I don't know, it's worth it. I don't know how long I'll be able to skate but I also really enjoy the other business of roller derby that I do. (pause) So it's worth it."

Impact on relationships

While earlier Emma admitted to underachieving at work, she did add on a serious note: "I don't really have a really good balance. It's really become difficult to fulfill my team commitments and also fulfill them with my other friends outside of derby." Emma, like others, noted that she has to be conscious of attending to her non-derby relationships because it is so easy to make derby your life. She continued, "Because there's always something I could be doing. Like, I could be volunteering to lay the track, or, you know – I enjoy it. I enjoy spending time with derby people and I enjoy doing things for the league." Kate similarly spoke of the conscious effort it takes to see non-derby people:

> I try to not just hang out with derby people all the time, but it definitely requires some effort every now and then, because there's always something to go to; a fundraiser, or a party, or a PR thing, and at some point you feel like, "Alright, that's it. No more derby things."

Jordan saw the pull of derby as being a bit of peer pressure: "I mean yeah there's a lot of peer pressure to make it your life. You know, like I have a lot of other shit in my life."

Finally, Natalie also spoke of the difficulty in maintaining non-derby relationships:

> It's tricky cause you can just get so involved with derby and not even realize it to the point where you're doing 40 or 50 hours a week of practicing and games and coaching and travelling and before you know it, you don't have any friends outside the derby community. It's kind of like you moved away, but you just moved into the derby warehouse down the street.

When I asked about either balance or about what their friends and family thought of their participation in roller derby, the women often shared that the time commitment took away from their relationships with their family and friends. Rae said:

> I've lost time with friends and family. That hurts. I miss out on family functions sometimes because of my commitment to derby. I have practice and I can't go. I consider it a job. A job that I love

and am passionate about, but it's work and sometimes it has inter-fered with that.

Andrea is on her last year of playing so she can focus her time back on her children: "I plan to make this my last skating season from the perspective of the time that it's taking and, obviously, I am a mom. I feel like my children have given me 3+ years to dedicate to this." Derby can also affect whether a woman will even have children. Natalie spoke of a single friend who wants to have children but derby has impacted her social life:

> One of my best friends that plays, she's thirty-seven, and she's like, "I want kids so bad, but I don't want to quit derby." And it's like what do you do, you're thirty-seven. [quoting her friend] "Whenever I find the love of my life, that's when I'll quit."

Natalie also echoed the sentiment that the time commitment can affect rela-tionships and create "derby widows." She said:

> Another thing that's a little sad about it is cause it is so time consuming and it's not our day job – you probably heard the term "derby widow." Over the years I've seen relationships come and go and a lot of relation-ships fail because of derby.

Despite their varying demographics, participants all agreed on one thing: derby requires a massive time commitment that impacts their non-derby relationships.

Impact on career?

In addition to impacting their personal relationships, the women also explained how roller derby has impacted their career and/or their profes-sional relationships. For some women, they either work from home or have a predictable 9-to-5 job so derby is easier to fit into their life. As two exam-ples, Lucy said: "It's generally a 9-to-5 office job . . . It's pretty stable – pretty predictable. I can work around that." Sarah agreed:

> I'm 45 and my daughter's 26 and so she's already grown and out of college, moved out. I live alone; I've worked from home and owned my own company. So by the time it's the afternoon and it's time to go to roller derby, I'm actually vibrant and ready to get out of the house and socialize.

Shannon achieves balance because she is able to work on derby stuff when work is slow: "When I'm not busy at work . . . I work on derby stuff there." Brooke is a graduate student who, like Ruth, said that derby has "taken a lot of time away from my studies, so it's sort of slowed me down school-wise (laughs)." However, though derby might add "an extra six months to a year" in graduate school, derby is still an important part of Brooke's life. She noted how lucky she is to have an advisor who supported her derby ambitions: "My professor, he's been very good to me. He actually came and watched me play a derby bout, so when I had one that was in town here he came, and he's been pretty supportive." She added that though he recognizes she is not as available to him as he might like, "he's been very accommodating to me."

Breaking her leg in derby made Emma realize the impact derby has had on her career goals:

> This broken leg has kind of made me think, like, "Ugh, I did want to do something different with my life work-wise," . . . So I think it does really take away my attention from other important life goals, maybe that I could be focusing on.

However, she adds, "But at the same time, it's so much fun and it is a goal for me to work on." I appreciated what Emma said about evaluating derby through a cost-benefit analysis and how we prioritize our goals: "I think about cost-benefit analysis, and I think about goals, and I just wonder what makes one goal more important than other goals. Why is . . . moving up in the ranks or even being more financially successful more important, you know?"

When I asked her how her colleagues have reacted to her playing derby, she said she has received a mixed reaction: "It's kind of a mixed bag. People like it insofar as they like it and are amused by it when it doesn't bump up against my work commitments." Emma, who works for a political party, added:

> But in an election scenario, or when the work starts to get more stress-ful or demanding, people have no time or patience for it, so in the past I've had to lie about going to practices (laughs). I've been like, "Oh, I have a very important meeting that I'm going to," but really I have my gear with me and I'm going to practice.

I then asked her how her colleagues have reacted to her broken leg, which has placed her on six weeks paid sick leave. She told me that everyone has been really nice and accommodating, even sending her flowers and chocolates. One of her bosses was at the bout where she broke her leg and:

> He keeps on emailing me because it was pretty disturbing for my friends to see me in agony, and to observe my leg in, like, a mangled condition. So they were deeply affected by it and, like, very shaken by it, so they're being really nice to me.

Other women mentioned their workplace was accommodating during their injuries, such as bringing them work so they could work from home while they recuperated. Julie said she only had to miss two days of work when she had surgery on her broken collar bone and then was still able to work while wearing a brace for three weeks and typing with her non-dominant hand. However, she was home-bound after having surgery to repair her torn ACL: "When I had my ACL surgery I was at home for about a week and a half, since I was on crutches I couldn't put weight on it for a while." During this time, she found her boss "was actually was very nice, she brought me work on Monday and Thursday and I was able to work from home for a little bit." Alexis's boss also brought her work to do following her second surgery for breaking her leg and dislocating her ankle, although her injury made it hard for her to be productive:

> So it ended up after both surgeries I took like a week off and they would just bring me work to do at home (laughs). And I was in like [a] pain-killer haze so I would do like 30 minutes of work and take like a 4-hour nap and then do a little more work.

Dana, in contrast, was unable to work from home while she recuperated from a dislocated thumb and a concussion. I asked how her workplace handled it and she responded that they were very supportive even though she could not do much work:

> It was a rough few months because I had a cast on my hand and I had a concussion so I could only work every half hour on the computer. So I'd work for a half hour and stare out the window for a half hour . . . I'm very blessed to have supervisors and coworkers that are OK with it.

Dana shared that when she lived in another major U.S. city, her employers were "not OK with it." In her experience, an employer's support is "really a hit or miss":

> I've had four different employers in my time playing derby and three out of the four have been really receptive of it. They've said, "OK,"

and I think they've kind of had the same thoughts as my grandmother, which is "How many injuries is it going to take before you stop?"

One of the reasons I was so interested in how coworkers and employers respond to one's participation in derby is because of the hypercompetitive, individualistic, neoliberal nature of the United States, combined with being a society where people, in particular low wage or hourly workers, do not always have access to affordable health insurance and healthcare. Many of the participants I interviewed were playing before the Patient Protection and Affordable Care Act ("Obamacare") became fully implemented and as such, did not necessarily have access to affordable healthcare, or if they did have access, their employer provided it, as is customary for millions of Americans. Therefore, a workplace's reaction to an employee's hobby, a hobby that is akin to a part-time job and which could render said employee unable to do their job, is a relevant question to ask. Skaters might be forced to reassess whether they can afford to remain in derby if attempts to repeal Obamacare are successful.

This brief discussion about employers' reactions previews the upcoming discussion about how pervasive and serious injuries are, to the extent that they invariably affect the family, friends, and coworkers in the women's lives.

The promise of injuries

Perhaps the obstacle that I found the most compelling, or the most obvious, is the threat of serious injury. Roller derby is a contact sport and injuries are so common that when learning of the women's experiences, it became necessary to create a separate spreadsheet to keep track of everyone's broken bones, torn ligaments, plus their surgeries, emergency room visits, casts, etc. While players from around the world risk serious injury when playing derby, I found it almost amusing that many of the American women would downplay injuries that many outsiders would consider very serious, especially in the United States, where access to affordable healthcare and health insurance can be rather dubious. The rest of the chapter examines the women's injuries, their reaction to their or others' injuries, as well as how loved ones react to their injuries.

"PCL 101"

While many know that tearing one's ACL, anterior cruciate ligament, or MCL, medial collateral ligament, are two knee injuries common to athletics, tearing the PCL, or posterior cruciate ligament, is one of the most common derby injuries. Two women described why lesser-known PCL injuries are so common in derby. Julie explained, "What I've heard from every skater who's ever had this injury and every doctor I've ever been to is that a PCL injury is extremely rare in almost all other sports but derby. So when you fall forward onto your knee in some way, that's when you tear that PCL in the back." Mary Ellen added, the injury is "because of the way we fall, we fall onto our knees. It's called a dashboard injury, same thing if you're sitting in a car and got reared ended and your knee slammed into your glove compartment. It's that force on the front of your knee that tears the back ligament. Anyway, PCL 101."

Maura discussed other common injuries, in addition to PCL injuries:

> Concussions are the big one and are a major problem because the helmets that most girls wear are not certified for the full-impact sport that we play . . . High-ankle sprains are also a big deal, and they take a long time to heal.

She notes that because the athletes are so focused on returning to play, they do not allow enough time for those sprains to heal, "so there's a risk of reinjury that's there." She continued, "we'll go through different themes in injuries, so lately it's been breaking the fibula (laughs). Which – it would be an ankle sprain, but it happens so quickly that it just breaks the bone instead."

"Breaking bones suck"

To the question, *Can you describe any injuries?* the women provided a catalog of injuries. Joanna, a mother of two daughters who also play derby, listed numerous series injuries including broken bones, torn ligaments, and even a third-degree muscle pull:

> I've broken a few bones here and there, I broke my leg, and I broke my hand in 3 places, I have 4 titanium screws! I've pulled both MCLs, both PCLs . . . I had a third degree groin pull, which was my full inner thigh from basically the top of my crotch to my knee was black and blue. It was just – it was horrible.

Some participants laughed when describing what many would consider to be serious injuries. For example, Audra laughed following a description of one injury: "A couple of weeks ago I got my jaw knocked out of its socket but that really wasn't that bad. It sounds a lot worse than it was (laughs)." Mary Ellen also laughed when listing her biggest injuries: "I've had two broken noses (laughs). The three of them together [she also tore her PCL], those are the big ones." Shannon laughed after recalling her struggle to straighten her wrist for six months, in addition to needing surgery to insert a plate and screws into her finger:

> Let's see. The shattered finger was the worst one, because I have a plate and six screws in my finger now because of it. I've blown out my knees a few times, I sprained my ankle in December, I cracked my sternum last year, I busted up my wrist pretty bad and couldn't move it – couldn't bend it or straighten it for six months. Yeah, that's all that came to mind. (laughs)

Like Shannon, Julie needed surgery to have a plate inserted, this time to repair her collar bone. Julie laughed loudly when recalling the severity of the break:

> I ruptured my ACL, I've had ACL replacement. And I've had like little minor stuff, but those are the only two [also a broken collar bone] that required surgery . . . the way it [her collar bone] was broken is one piece was so far back that it wouldn't knit together so they had to put a plate in it. (laughs)

Alexis is another player whose injuries necessitated surgery. In fact, one injury required two surgeries to fix:

> I've had stupid little things like jammed fingers or pretty gnarly bruises but definitely breaking my leg [and dislocating her ankle] was my most severe injury . . . I had to have two different surgeries to like, I had like a plate pin put in and they took one of the really big pins out, so you know, it was an excruciating journey.

My takeaway from the interviews is that serious injuries are the norm, not the exception. Thus, the prospect of serious injury is a major consideration of whether one should remain in the sport. At the same time, I could sense, from their laughter or their tone, that some participants recited their litany of injuries with a sense of pride.

"Did I just break my neck?"

Some of the women discussed scary injuries that happened to them or teammates: Julie described her "scariest injury by far," when she sprained her neck:

> As I hit the ground and I snapped by neck, and I kind of just laid there for a second thinking, "Oh my God, did I just break my neck?" And

then I didn't want them to call the jam because of me, because if you're on the ground for, I don't know, three seconds or more, the referees will just call the jam, and then you're out for three jams. So I got up, and I said, "Okay, it must not be broken because I can still skate," but it was just awful. It hurt so bad.

Helena, a nurse, described an injury she witnessed that initially was not being taken seriously by a physician's assistant at the bout, who told the player to take some Celebrex, an anti-inflammatory. Helena said she was standing there thinking: "She can't close her mouth. Like, she's not able to bring her jaw together and she's having trouble talking . . . She needs to go to the ER." Helena decided to call over to the local emergency room to see about the wait time: "I found out later that she did have a broken jaw, they [the ER] ended up transferring her over to one of the trauma hospitals to have her jaw wired." This player had just returned from another injury and "that was the final straw. She never did come back to derby after that, so (pause) it was pretty intense."

Rae had to be carried out on a backboard after spraining her neck. When I asked Natalie to describe her injuries, she replied, "I actually have a really good one." She meant she had a really good story, but in reality, she almost died from her injury: "Somebody hit me in the chest, which was a totally legal hit, but it punctured my lungs (laughs) . . . and so I had a tiny little rip and it was just seeping air." She said she had an "air bubble in my throat starting to restrict my airway and I went to the urgent care and said 'Something's wrong with my throat and it feels weird.'" They took an x-ray and told her "If you had waited 20 more minutes, you'd have died. I was like, 'AH!'" They told her, "Don't ever play roller derby again or any sport where you can get hit in the chest," which to her felt "like kind of a death sentence." Not only did she continue playing derby, she in fact moved to a major city to try out (successfully) for one of the best teams in the world. Of the injury, she said, "It really lit a fire under me that life is short." While life may be short, she will be dealing with derby's effects on her body for years to come. She added: "I think about my body, I can't bend my knees . . . I haven't been able to bend my knees for two years."

Dana was another participant who mentioned a few injuries, including a torn PCL, a minor concussion, and a sprained ankle. But then Dana also described more serious injuries, including a concussion that actually changed her eyesight and herniated disks that made it hard to stand or walk:

In my farewell game [before moving across the country to join a new league], I got a concussion to the eye. So her [the opponent] shoulder went into my face and that changed my eyesight and that was a really awful concussion.

While still recovering from that concussion, she joined a new league in a new city. In her second game:

I herniated two disks in my back, where my spine meets my pelvis. So that took me out an entire season, and it was incredibly hard to walk or to support or stand for long period of time. And that's something that I still deal with, you know, it's still painful and if I get hit the wrong way or fall the wrong way, I'm out for a week until it calms down.

She mentioned dislocating her thumb:

This past summer I dislocated my thumb and was in a cast for three months because you have to get all the fluid back in your joints. Basically if you look at the thumb muscle where your hand goes into your wrist there's fluid there that needs to be restored and so I needed to be immobilized in order to restore fluid and so that my muscles wouldn't get messed up. That sucked.

She concluded her recitation of injuries with: "I think that's it. I have not broken a bone. In my whole time I haven't broken a bone. Knock on wood, I haven't broken a bone." Incredulously, even Dana, who had some of the worst injuries in terms of the sheer number of serious injuries requiring long recoveries or permanent damage, ended this section of our interview with, "Knock on wood, I haven't broken a bone."

"Nothing serious"

To me, as an outsider, what shocked me, in addition to the brutal injuries, was how conditioned some of the women were to rate their injuries as *relative* to other players. Participants would say, "Nothing serious," or "It sounds worse than it was," while describing what I bet many outside of sports would consider to be serious injuries. Suzy, before listing a variety of injuries said: "In TOTAL, I think I've come out on the good side of injuries." Her injuries across her (to date) five-year career include a shoulder muscle detaching, a partial tear of her meniscus, a broken nose and a broken thumb. Suzy, like others, would talk casually about needing to do physical therapy, or thinking an injury was not too serious if it was non-surgical: "I broke my nose last season which was non-surgical as well and that only took me out for a couple weeks. And then I also broke my thumb but I just, I just skated through that, so that didn't take me out at all (laughs)."

On the other hand, measuring one's injuries relative to others makes sense because the injuries often take place in front of each other in a practice, scrimmage, or bout. Andrea mentioned thinking she was tough playing through a jammed finger, until she realized others were playing with broken bones:

> I remember at the very first couple practices, I jammed my finger . . . and I wore, like, a little brace on my index finger, and I kept going to practice, and I felt, like, "Oh, look at me, I'm injured and I'm still practicing. I'm so tough."

She quickly learned: "Well that was nothing, of course. There are girls who have had broken arms, with casts on their arms and they still put their skates on, gear up, and they practice." The takeaway from seeing teammates play through their injuries is "not giving up." She continued, "Because you don't want to punk out. You don't want to look like, 'Oh gosh, I'm weak.' So you continue to push through, which I think can be beneficial at times."

"The most badass story"

For participants, the contact nature of the sport is a draw to them, both because they like hitting other players, but also because of a certain kind of pride they feel from getting through an injury, which at times includes playing injured. Joanna, who had just returned to playing from a broken leg, broke her hand a week or two later. She said:

> I was mad as hell. And I told the doctor, "Put a cast on." Because if I have a cast on, I can play [in a bout the next day]. And he's like, "You can't have a cast on. We can't do that. It's too soon."

Joanna said she lasted a week before demanding the doctor put a cast on her arm:

> I said "Either you put a cast on, or I'm going to buy some plaster of Paris and I'll do it myself!" Alright, so he put it on. So I played, I had to wear the cast for 5 weeks, so I played for 5 weeks, and that was an adjustment, because I couldn't tie my own skates.

Joanna is not the only one to do whatever she could to get back to playing. Jordan, who had a few injuries involving ligament tears in her knee, obsessively did her physical therapy to rehabilitate her knee: "I obsessively did my physio exercises and you know, a lot of people get pretty lazy on that (laughs) but I was pretty motivated to get back to practice and get back to playing. And I'm like miserable (laughs) not doing it [derby]."

Emma shared that her injury inducts her into a proud tradition in her league:

> But I happen to be part of a proud tradition, because [her home team] are known for a number of things: We're known for having the most hardware in our bodies. (laughs)

Additionally, stories of toughness in the face of incredible injuries tend to spread. One woman, Julie, told me the story of how she played through the jam despite breaking her collar bone: "(laughs) My very first bout I broke my collar bone (laughs)." She explained that "It's the most badass story that I'll ever have in my entire life" because it was not only her first bout, but it was her very first jam. They put her in as jammer and "I went out I broke my collar bone about half way around my first lap, but I got back up, I got through the pack, I got lead jammer with my broken collar bone and I called [the jam]." Unbelievably, a previous interviewee had already told me that story. I told Julie that and she replied, "It's pretty much the greatest thing I've ever done."

"I was absolutely terrified"

For some of the women, the pride comes from getting over their initial fear of derby and getting hit. Andrea explained, "That was actually the scary part (laughs). Just the full-contact of it and thinking, 'Oh my Gosh, I'm going to get hit and it's going to hurt.'" She said that you learn how to give and take a hit, and how to fall:

> But once you learn to fall and feel confident in your skill, it just becomes second nature and you're okay with it. There's still some hits that hurt harder than others, some girls hit harder than others, but you learn to kind of absorb those hits or hit back versus just waiting for the hit, if that makes sense.

Brooke echoed the sentiment that beginning derby can be "terrifying": "It was terrifying. I mean the whole thing. I was absolutely terrified." She said that both her dad and her boss would tell her she would get hurt a lot and break her leg. However, she wanted to challenge herself by trying out. Now, two years into her playing career, she said,

> And I'm still scared now, like I get a little worried that I'll get hurt real bad, but my confidence is much higher now knowing how to fall and

different things, so there's still the chance that I'll break my leg, but I guess I'll have to deal with that.

Andrea discussed the tension between liking the physical contact but feeling genuinely sorry if she injures another player:

> Last night I hit this girl in the nose, and BECAUSE I'm a mother, and because she's younger, I kept looking back at her in the jam, because I knew I hit her so hard, and I kept thinking, "Oh gosh, she's going to have a bloody nose."

Andrea apologized after the jam to the still mad-opponent: "After the jam I looked at her, and I was like, 'I am so sorry' . . . it's sincere . . . I mean, you feel horrible, but it's derby." She added: "But it's a fun sport. I mean, yeah . . . when I knocked my first girl down, I was like, 'YES, I just knocked her out.' So it's really rewarding at the same time."

Sarah, in some ways, had a different reaction to her injuries. She tore her PCL and her MCL, separated her shoulder, broke her tailbone, and had a concussion. She attributed her serious injuries to her inexperience with derby combined with her history of skating. With a figure skating national champion for a sibling, Sarah grew up skating. As a result, she very quickly found herself skating among veteran skaters:

> I think that was probably a bad thing because I didn't know derby yet, how to take a hit, give a hit, so I was kind of put in situations where I skated well enough to be there but I didn't play derby well enough to be there.

She responded by pulling back and moving herself down to the C team, where she planned to stay awhile until she progressed at derby skills: "So I've kind of taken control of that and stepped back . . . I'm happy where I'm at [regarding her progression of skills] and want to stay on the C team for a year."

Dana, whose injuries included an eyesight-altering concussion and herniated disks, explained that she rejected back surgery because the risk of never being able to walk again was too high. Doctors told her she

> could have surgery but there was a 30 percent chance that I wouldn't walk and that was 30 percent too high. If it had been like five I would have done it . . . it's [her back] something that I know I have to live with. And I'm OK with that because I can walk and I can play and I can live a fruitful life with some modification.

I asked her if knowing about her serious injuries, if she could go back in time, would she still choose derby? She responded: "Oh yeah, totally."

"Reality sets in": the sobering element of injuries

While some find pride in how they play through injuries, or come back from them, others find injuries to be a sobering element of the sport. Maya, who had been skating for three months, told me she was glad that she did not tell people at work "right off the bat" because all the injuries she is witnessing is turning her off of derby: "The more I get into it and seeing the injuries, I'm PROBABLY not going to keep with it." Or she is also considering not getting drafted to a team on purpose: "That way I can still join league practices and scrimmage with the girls but I guess I'm just going to have to figure out how tough I am." She described a serious injury at a recent scrimmage that was so severe that "we all sort of stepped back." A teammate broke her ankle pretty seriously and required surgery. For Maya, whose job as a civil engineer requires physical movement, her teammate's injury gave her pause: "My career demands physical movement so I kind of, it was the one thing so far where reality sunk in, you know. You have to be very careful and defensive. It is a serious risk you take." Sarah agreed that it takes an injury to force you evaluate derby's role in your life: "It takes an injury or something that opens your eyes."

Others find that their injury reveals how important derby is to them. Maude had a two-month injury when she sprained her ankle badly. She realized she went from seeing her friends four nights a week and suddenly was lonely: "I'd get home from work and I was used to seeing all these people, like, four times a week every night . . . And then just nothing. I'd just watch TV all alone. I got kind of depressed, absolutely."

Though she said breaking her leg was "an excruciating journey" because of the two surgeries it took to fix, Alexis also said breaking her leg was "the best thing that ever happened" to her because it solidified how important derby was to her. When she came back:

> I was WAY better than I was before. I was FASTER, I was STRONGER and I spent a lot of time [while injured] reading rules and watching derby and stuff and (pause) my game was just exponentially better . . . I don't know that I would have been as committed if I wasn't injured like that.

Dana saw this ability – or inability – to return from an injury to be an interesting part of one's psychology:

> Some of these girls are like "Oh my God I can't handle this, and I want to play but I can't," and it's really the psychology of you coming back

from an injury and how they handle it and if they come back or if they just shut down and stay home all day. It's really interesting.

Though some women see the injuries as sobering, others see their own injuries as solidifying their commitment to derby, and others defend the risk they take by arguing that one can get injured anywhere. Joanna recalled:

> I think any sport you play, you can get hurt. I mean, a friend of mine, who actually plays roller derby with us, she broke her ankle playing kickball . . . [at least] I hurt my leg and I've got a cool story to go with it!

Ruth concurred:

> I have a baby at home and someone said to me "Isn't it kind of irresponsible if your kid needs you and you get hurt?" And I think you get hit by a bus on the street . . . You just have to live your life and not be scared of injury otherwise we'd never do anything.

Ruth, like others, noted that this pushback against their participation often comes from well-intentioned family, friends, and coworkers. While earlier I shared quotes discussing problems arising from the enormous time commitment, participants also described family and friends who dislike going to bouts or who struggle seeing an injury occur. Dana has had boyfriends refuse to come see her bout, and who had trouble being "intimate" because her body was covered in bruises:

> Oh yeah, I had boyfriends who refused to come to games because they didn't want to see me hurt and didn't like it when I would go and try to be intimate and have bruises on me, they would be like "You need to stop." And I'm like "no." and so it was either roller derby or this dude, and I was like "I'm picking roller derby." Which is kind of awesome.

She added that her experience is not unique: "But there are a lot of girls like that that have lost relationships over the sport." Maya agreed that people just do not understand how these women would put their bodies through such pain, asking her: "Why would you go out and intentionally hurt yourself?" She admitted: "You can't explain it until you're in it. (laughs) Yeah, it's a EUPHORIC BRUISE (laughs). Like you're angry someone hit you and you're excited." In summary, listening to participants recall their injuries left me with a sense that while painful, scary, expensive, and body-altering and even life-threatening, being injured instilled a sense of pride.

Their ability to withstand the pain and return from an injury only further cemented their credibility within the derby community.

This chapter examined what should be three major hurdles to playing derby: the steep financial and time commitments, and the very real threat of serious injury. To those unaffiliated with derby, the thought of a 20 hour per week commitment, expensive and dangerous hobby seems unrealistic, even "foolish," but the women enumerated a variety of benefits they gain from playing. The next two chapters examine such benefits. Chapter 3 focuses on benefits such as improved self-esteem, confidence and body image, camaraderie and fostering female friendships, and the thrill of competition. Chapter 4 examines the role of the derby persona, sometimes referred to as the alter ego, which women described overwhelmingly as a positive element to the sport.

Reference

Wilkie, D. (2017). Workplace burnout at 'epidemic proportions' Retrieved from: www.shrm.org/resourcesandtools/hr-topics/employee-relations/pages/employee-burnout.aspx

3 Benefits of playing roller derby

The previous chapter examined three major hurdles to playing roller derby: the large time and financial commitments and the promise of serious, often expensive, injuries. I now consider the benefits, or the reasons why women play roller derby, despite those hurdles. Specifically, participants attribute numerous benefits to derby, including improved health as well as developing certain aspects of their personality, especially confidence and self-esteem. Many women also shared how derby feeds their need for a contact sport in their life, especially what some women referred to as an "outlet for their aggression." Participants also cited building a large circle of supportive and diverse female friends, a first for many of the women, as a major benefit to playing derby.

"The best shape of my life"

Improved health was a benefit nearly all of the women mentioned. For example, Alexis stated: "I'm exhausted but I'm also in the best shape of my life." Some of the women specified that their weight loss was due to derby. Dana said: "When I initially started I dropped about 50 pounds." Bridgett, who when asked how derby has benefitted her life, said excitedly: "Oh my gosh, I love derby so much. I could talk about it for hours," articulated how derby has improved her body: "I think I've lost about ten pounds and I'm toned up amazingly. Like, people have noticed that I've toned up all because of derby." Many of the women discussed ways derby has improved their body, such as improving their muscle tone. For Andrea, derby has helped her manage her weight as she hit 40 years old:

> Well, obviously being forty, I start to hit that hormone zone (laughs). You know, some of my friends my age have started to gain weight, and I just haven't noticed that with derby. I think my fitness level has been able to stay up.

Joanna told me derby has helped her daughter, who also participates in derby, lose the weight she gained following her parents' divorce:

> My eldest daughter, she's a little bit bigger girl. The separation, the divorce, did a lot to her. She binge ate a lot, and she's gained a lot of weight since, so derby's helped her to lose some of that.

While some shared their weight loss, others discussed the impact on their physical health more broadly, including developing habits that are more positive. For example, Basma decreased the amount she drinks because it would conflict with goals she has set as an athlete:

> Ya know, I do drink still, but not like a was before I had found derby. I spend more time at the track and training and things like that with my spare time. Back then I would just be out partying and doing things that [would now] hurt me being an athlete and keep me from moving forward as quickly and getting to where I ultimately want to go with derby.

Sarah said derby has improved her fitness, important as she has a sedentary job:

> Oh, I mean it's benefitted me in so many ways. I mean just increasing my activity level that much because I have a sedentary work from home job and my huge problems with my back, they call it computer hunch. I have to go to the chiropractor.

Maude realized just how much derby had benefitted her health when she injured her ankle and was "off skates":

> I found when I was off-skate and when my ankle was injured, waking up was a lot harder, which doesn't make sense since I was getting more sleep. But I became a bum. So it keeps me energized. It gives me something to look forward to.

In addition to weight loss or improved physical health, various women spoke of how the healthy lessons learned and habits formed will stay with them after derby. Alexis said that she while she always considered herself to be physically active, she will continue being motivated to eat healthy and build strength: "It's going to be a lifelong lesson to focus on what I'm eating. I've always been pretty healthy but trying to build muscle and kind of a routine of strength." Meagan likewise will carry the benefits with her:

> I feel like I've gotten a lot out of it, physically and health wise, and I think that will be the thing that stays with me the most because I will feel like I've actually done something for myself (pause) to stay healthy . . . Maybe it can be a continuous thing (pause) just to remind myself to make good choices health-wise. Because I feel like I'm more conscious of the things I eat, with cross training and everything, so I think that's what's going to stay with me in my mind.

Julie, who, as "a skinny person" blessed with "good genes," hated sports and gym class, said derby changed her perspective on health and wellness:

> It's [derby] just really changed my whole perspective on being in shape and taking good care of myself and eating the right foods. And I just feel so much healthier now than I did 20 years ago. So that's, like, one of the biggest things to me.

Twenty-five-year-old Maude sees the healthful and youthful-looking older women in her league as a positive depiction of what she can look forward to as she ages: "Everybody in derby, no matter what their age, they just look like five and ten years younger. And it's incredible knowing (laughs), when I'm their age I'm still going to look young and awesome."

Numerous women used the term *focus* to highlight the direction or consciousness that derby has given them. Rae referred to this focus as how she coped with a multiple sclerosis diagnosis. She said there are two responses to such news:

> Either you curl up in a ball and you just focus on that as opposed to focusing on the good in life and things that you can do. I fell into that because I consider myself a big fighter . . . and I do feel like keeping moving and keeping active and staying healthy and eating healthy helps me keep it in check.

She later added: "I feel like nothing's going to stop me except for myself playing the sport." Though such a serious diagnosis might keep some women from derby, Rae said her doctor actually encouraged her to keep playing: "My doctor told me to just keep doing it because it's something that I love and am passionate about and it's keeping me healthy."

Others similarly discussed the ways derby has increased their focus on other areas of their life. Bridgett, who earlier in her interview explained how derby helped lift her depression after losing two aunts in close succession, illustrated how derby's benefits spilled over into her entire life:

> And derby just helped balance me mentally and physically, because I was so depressed for a while. It's made me more focused, more organized so I can balance my time out a little better. I manage my money better because I have to pay dues, and I have to keep up on my equipment, pay for uniforms . . . And it kind of bleeds into all aspects of life, really.

Brooke, who did not join derby specifically to lose weight, discussed the focus derby has brought to her health. Before derby she "was sluggish and tired all the time," whereas now, derby has: "gotten me more focused on living a better life. Now I eat better, I get more exercise on the side than I used to, so I exercise on top of just training roller derby." Like Bridgett, Brooke shared that derby helped lift her depression, in addition to adding muscle tone:

> I'm probably the same weight [as before], but I was bigger because I was fat, and I didn't do a lot, I was depressed, you know, it's just kind of like every day I'd go to school and then I'd come home, and it was like, "UGH."

A few of the women shared that part of their motivation stems not from wanting to be skinnier, but for how their strong bodies can propel them in the sport. Some merely described this as motivation to be better at derby or as meeting the goals they set for themselves. However, Brooke detailed specifically how being in shape improves her game: "So I can run, I can get through the pack's center (laughs). I can get around the track easier. I don't get tired after doing, like, five laps or being chased down (laughs)."

Sarah, who lives and plays in Colorado, was unsurprised by derby's success in a state that prides itself on its physical activity. However, seeing derby's impact in more stereotypically sedentary states surprised her:

> This is our lifestyle, so it didn't surprise me to walk into derby here in Colorado and see women my age. It surprises me when we play Iowa and I see women my age who have never played a sport and never played derby. That does surprise me . . . because you see other parts of the country where it's literally women of all ages

with no background at all and not in shape and saying, "OK well I'm going to play derby."

Brooke described derby as opening a "whole new world" she did not know existed. Sarah similarly described derby as "enhancing your life": "You look forward to playing and after you play you feel better. You feel better about yourself, you feel better physically. I mean it really just enhances your life. It doesn't take away from your life." She compares derby to the runner's high that distance runners get and then says: "You get that derby high from you feeling really good about you always improving and getting better and playing on the next level of team and our team goes to the championship bouts every year. It just has that element where it adds good things to your life."

Overall, participants expressed that derby impacted their physical and mental health in life-changing ways. This discussion of health benefits segues into the next section, which outlines how derby is welcoming to women of all body shapes, a fact that many women find both welcoming and empowering.

"There's a place for everyone"

Because of the three different positions (jammer, blocker, and pivot), derby, as with some other sports, benefits from having women of various body types playing. As Brooke explained,

> The thing about derby is that there's a place for everyone in it. You know, if you're a big girl, there's a place for you. If you're a small girl, there's a place for you . . . And that's one of the best parts about it.

Eliza echoed this sentiment when we were discussing junior derby:

> You've got super skinny and petite girls, then you've got big girls who are muscular or – you've got short, tall, stocky, skinny, I'm astounded by how many body types are in there, because a lot of people, when they hear derby, they think, "Oh, it's just a bunch of really big girls," and I'm like, "Nope, it's everything across the board."

When I commented that it is a great sport for young women to have, Eliza added: "Oh yeah, and to actually have role-models who actually don't look like toothpicks." This appreciation for various body types helped the women feel more comfortable with their own body, and their own skills.

Sarah discussed hearing a teammate give a talk and appreciated how she framed the relationship between derby and body image:

> [My teammate said] "You know I'm not a model. I don't have a perfect body but my body does things on the track that other girls' bodies can't do." I thought that was very eloquently stated, that she loved her body because when she plays roller derby she can do amazing things with her body that many people can't do.

Brooke, upon seeing a wide variety of body types at a tournament, reflected: "This is wonderful because I don't have to feel fat, I don't have to feel bad about myself in any way. Derby just makes me feel so good about my body, and I think that it's important to women." She feels so "uplifted" by the diverse bodies that she plans to expose her daughter to derby and would be "so supportive" if she decided to take up the sport.

One of the reasons different body types are welcome in derby is due to the nature of the contact sport. As Sarah said, it doesn't matter how in shape she is if someone who outweighs her by a hundred pounds hits her:

> I'm more lean and a typically jammer build and I have to say some of the bigger girls when they hit me, it doesn't matter how strong I am and how many weights I've lifted. When someone who weighs a hundred pounds more than me hits me, I'm going out. You know? They hit me, I'm going to bounce.

In contrast, Maura shared the story of being told she is rather small when she showed up, but nevertheless was still welcomed. "When I started, everyone looked at me and were like, 'Well you're kind of small.' (laughs) Small for derby, but it doesn't matter what size you are, you can go and do this."

Madeline explained how derby gives her confidence to appreciate her body: "It's given me a lot more confidence. It's given me the idea that I don't have to be this super super thin ideal woman. I can be a little bit bigger. I can be stronger. I'm perfectly happy with it."

Increased empowerment of their bodies is just one way the women reported increased confidence. The next section explores how derby improved participants' confidence and self-esteem.

"Something changes in them on the track"

Numerous participants discussed the increase in self-confidence as a direct result of playing roller derby. Bridgett was drawn to derby in the first place after watching a bout and seeing the confidence in the athletes: "It's the fact that the women look so confident on the track and the slightly glamorous aspect of it. I mostly just wanted that confidence that these girls have." When I asked her later what she believes her biggest takeaway from playing derby will be, Bridgett replied: "The self-confidence I have in myself now. It seriously has boosted me up so much that I think it's one thing that I'll always and forever have with me." Brooke gave the same reply when asked what she will take away from her time playing derby: "It's given me a lot of confidence. Confidence in my body and just in life in general. Given me an edge to become more outgoing because, I don't know, I just feel better about myself, you know?"

For some of the women, the fact that they tried out for derby and are finding success led to increased confidence. Alexis described this pride in accomplishing something that initially scared her. Of the benefits of derby, she stated:

Definitely helping to develop my confidence I guess (pause). I was never really outgoing or anything like that before. I mean, I wasn't like a social recluse but I was scared to try stuff and scared to talk to people and afraid of failure (laughs). So roller derby was like the first thing in my life that I was like, "I'm pretty sure I will fail at it because I don't understand it (laughs) but I want to do it."

Rae is always surprised by the number of women who initially say that they cannot do derby who then are transformed in their first bout:

That's the biggest thing that surprises me – because I've seen so many women try out for derby and [they say] "I don't know. I don't know if I can do that. I don't think I could get out there and be hit or hit somebody." They try out, they train really hard, and then they have their first bout. Something changes in them on the track. They can do it.

To Rae, this transformation into self-confident athletes has been the "coolest" and most surprising aspect of derby:

That's been the most surprising thing – is just that confidence that it exudes in women. They get out there and they become someone completely different. It's like they've found something that they never realized that they had. I think that's the coolest thing that I've experienced and the most surprising.

Madeline recalled moments where she and her teammates discussed this "derby confidence" as a reminder of what skaters must overcome to play and how derby empowers them to see other problems from new perspectives. She elaborated: "After you've been smashed around by people who expect you to get up and just keep taking it, most things in life seem pretty tame compared to that."

Other participants noted how the confidence has spilled over into their work lives. Audra reflected:

> It's given me this sense of peace, and this strength it's given me has made it – has made other parts of my life easier for once. Because, you know, I feel better about myself. I feel better about everything (laughs). I feel like it helps sort of give me focus, make me confident, be more at ease with other parts of my life.

Likewise, Alexis specified how her newfound confidence affected her at work:

> [Derby] helped develop my character at work. In terms of confidence to do projects or talk to people who are difficult personalities (laughs) or things like that. I was very non-confrontational (pause) when I started this job six years ago. I couldn't even talk on the phone when someone else was in the room. That's how shy I was (laughs). But now, I run a whole region and I tell people that they have to do stuff or they're fired (laughs). It's a BIG change from how I was.

For some women, derby gave them the confidence to make changes to their lives outside of derby. Sarah left her job and started her own company because of confidence gained from derby:

> My job was really stressful, and I think [derby] gave me the confidence to say, "You know I really can change my life." And I opened up my own company and took control of what days look like. I still do the same job, I just do it for myself now instead of a corporation, so it gives me a lot of freedom.

Lucy described the way her newfound confidence pulled her out of her rut, improving her emotional and mental health:

> Confidence wise – I have found something that I am comfortable in. I think in general I regained the confidence that I hadn't had for a long time. I was kind of in a rut for a long time. That is a very big positive element that [derby] has provided for me. Because of all that, my mental and emotional health has improved as well. All of those different elements.

Self-confidence is not the only personality benefit the women experience thanks to roller derby; many participants also cited benefits related to aggression, often referring to derby as an "outlet."

"It's just like therapy"

Bridgett said a major reason she plays derby is to have an outlet for her anger and aggression: "For me at least, part of the reason I do it is cause, also, on top of all those [other benefits], it's also an incredible outlet for frustration and anger and aggression and it just, it's like therapy." Bridgett added that women need outlets for their aggression just as men do, and to think otherwise is simply outdated:

> Well I would say it's just kind of foolish, this outdated idea that we're all these little delicate flowers to take care of . . . Women need an outlet, women have just as much aggression as men do and they just really need an outlet.

Mary Ellen echoed Bridgett's view of derby as an outlet:

> It's really an outlet. It really is, and not just for "Oh, I'm mad, I'm going to go play roller derby and get some of my aggression out." That's part of it, but I mean it truly is an escape from your everyday life. If you're happy, you get on the track and you just have fun with everyone. If you're mad about something that happened in your day, you get out there and you just skate it out, I mean it really is a release.

Mary Ellen shared that it is this release that keeps her tied to derby: "So I think when I've taken periods of time off that's what I'm missing and that's what's always kind of forcing me to go back." Joanna, who engages in customer service every day with her own company, said: "So it is really nice to have that out . . . I get a lot of aggression out! Any and all frustrations I take with me on the track and I use that to power myself on the track too." She added: "Some people that have known me for a lot of years have said that I'm a much nicer person since I started playing roller derby." Later in her interview, she added: "Just having that release to get any and all aggression out. I think that's been the biggest benefit for me personally." Lynn uses the word *cathartic* instead of "outlet" to describe the pull of derby: "Basically it's just a hell of a lot of fun . . . It's kind of cathartic. If you've been having a bad day to, you know, bump into some girls and skate it out." Rae acknowledges "it sounds bad to say," but agrees that for her, derby is anger management: "It's anger management . . . you come to practice. You could have the worst day ever and you just go and scrimmage and you get hit and people are hitting you and it's just . . . I don't know. It's nice." Rae said this appreciation for the aggression derby gives them is not one sided; in fact, it helps build camaraderie:

> This sounds weird, but when I get hit really hard, I'm always like, "That was a really awesome hit," to whoever hit me . . . We appreciate that about each other. It's a good thing. It sounds twisted, but it is a really good thing.

Meagan also mentioned the combination of being physical with each other at practice and in bouts and yet maintaining their camaraderie: "The aggression is a nice part of it too (laughs), because we all play the sport and then we all go out and have a beer together so it's good camaraderie (pause) with anybody you meet." Bridgett agreed:

> Of course I like hitting people (laughs) on skates. I mean, you have to do it right, but I think this is the one sport where you can go and hit someone and then hug them and be like, "You did a really great job in the game tonight," you know? "That hit you made was amazing," and you're just friends as soon as the game's over.

Basma appreciates derby as an outlet for letting women explore their aggressive side, but qualifies that derby is just as much skill as aggression, perhaps explaining how skaters are able to maintain friendships while engaging in such a physical sport:

> I just think that it's really amazing how we [women] finally have a sport where you can be so aggressive – and it's a different kind of aggression . . . You definitely want to hit as hard as you can and have the skill that you need to be out there. But nobody ever goes out there intentionally to hurt anybody else. But you want to hit as hard as you can and be as powerful as you can while you are out there. Sometimes that power is more skilled knowledge than it is physical, if that makes sense.

Sarah, who had extensive sporting experience prior to finding derby, thinks the physical contact is a huge draw for women:

> I'm so sorry that I didn't find roller derby ten years ago, but I'm glad I have all that sports history to make the comparisons. Nothing compares to playing a female contact sport because I played every sport known – they were not contact sports. So I truly believe the fascination

is that it's a contact sport – that you get to hit and you get to have that experience that you never got to have before.

Maura concurred: "I don't know what the deal is, but I like hitting people (laughs). I like that aggression, I guess, and . . . [hitting is] way more fun for me (laughs)."

For some outsiders, the idea – or the scene – of women knocking each other around in a sporting competition one minute and hugging and socializing the next may be hard to believe. Yet nearly every woman mentioned the expanded social circle, and specifically the close, female friendships, as a major benefit to roller derby.

"With open arms"

Maya, who described herself as shy, reported that derby has brought many friendships into her life: "It's definitely brought some new friendships into my life, so that's great." Another self-described shy skater, Meagan attributed derby for helping her to open up:

> When I first started I was really shy. I've always been shy as a kid and everything. And then when I came to the sport, I just felt like there were all these women around me that were here for all the same goal. And I felt like I could open up to them, so it definitely brought me out of my shell.

Bridgett also felt welcomed by everyone: "They accepted all the new girls with open arms. I've made, like, fifty friends, all of whom know my name – maybe not my real name, but they all know my name."

Brooke and Maura mentioned an expanded social circle. Brooke said: "I've got a couple really good friends that I made through derby and who I hang out with on a regular basis. So that's really good." Maura similarly articulated: "Definitely my friend network, my social network, has expanded substantially."

A few of the women elaborated on how the derby network helps them in their non-derby lives, from helping each other move to rides to the airport. Alexis illustrated:

> People have been super helpful about helping me move or helping me figure out where to go and get my license and stuff like that, especially with a league as big as [ours], there's a million resources even if you're just like, "Hey does anyone know a lawyer who's familiar with this stuff," [and] there's 10 people in the league who right away respond to your e-mail and say, "yea I've got a guy." (laughs)

Madeline had a similar experience with her league: "Most of [the women] will actually [say] 'Hey, I'll drive you to the airport; I'll do this for you. I'll do that for you.' It becomes more of a sisterhood than anything." Andrea's league actually has big and little sisters to help mentor new skaters: "We also have big sisters and little sisters, so we take that family atmosphere inside of the community. If you have questions, you have someone that you can go to." Helena also found her league to be very supportive and inclusive:

> They were just such a supportive group of women to each other. If one of them was getting married, they would help out with the wedding. If somebody was having financial issues or things like that, they were very understanding and they would help that person out.

"I've never done well with women"

A number of women explained that building female friendships through derby has been especially impactful in their life because, for various reasons, they previously had few to no female friends. A common reason women gave was they just naturally got along better with men. Joanna is one such woman. She recounted:

> I was never one that had a lot of girlfriends growing up. I always played better with boys. And even in the military, I had way more guy friends than I had girlfriends. So it was nice to actually have some girls to hang out with, stuff like that, which was awesome.

Rae was 30 before she experienced the advantages of female friends: "I have always had guy friends for the most part. And I was about 30 when I started playing derby and I realized the importance of needing more feminine relationships in my life I guess." Dana likewise had few female friends because she felt she had little in common with women: "I think I've always had concerning relationships with other women, just because I don't fit the stereotype of the 'lip gloss and go shopping' or 'let's go get our nails done.' . . . I just didn't want to do it." Jordan described how derby forced her to adjust her stereotypes of women as crazy while teaching her how to interact better with women:

> I think [derby] has helped me a lot to have better relationships with women. I mostly have hung out with guys and found women a bit OVERBEARING (laughs). So I think that it's exposed me to a lot more, a lot of different types of women and (pause) taught me a bit

more about how to interact (laughs) with women and not immediately assume they're all going to be crazy. (laughs)

Mary Ellen had female friendships in high school and college, but not since graduating. She appreciates how these new friendships have expanded her children's social circle as well:

> For me personally, I've never done well with women, I don't know what it is, but I haven't had any close women friends since I was in high school and college, so that is the second-best benefit for me. Making a lot of friends in the area, and a lot of moms with children my kids' age, that we do stuff together all the time.

Kimberly described her lack of friends as due to her family moving a lot as a child:

> My dad was in the military so we moved a lot when I was a kid so I don't have like a hometown and I don't have childhood friends. But I think with derby I've made friendships that are actually going to stick, which is exciting.

Later in the interview, she also concluded that her lack of female friends was due to her athletic interests:

> I wasn't normally the kind of girl who had a lot of female friends. Because I was athletic, I tended to have a lot of male friends and now I have this circle of really close girlfriends which is something I've never had before. It's really a new thing for me.

Kimberly also raised an interesting point. Because of the way her league set up travel and home teams, she often bouts competitively, in front of large crowds, against women she always trains with:

> One of the interesting things we have, since our league has three teams, whenever our travel team is playing a home bout, our two home teams play against each other. So like three times a season, I play against girls that I train with constantly.

She recalled that for other physical sports she has played, like rugby and hockey, you compete against strangers and if you lose, you want nothing to do with the other team. Derby is physical just like these other sports, and yet, following a bout where she "puts everything out there", she parties with and even babysits the kids of these teammates/competitors: "I competitively put everything out there, play as hard as I can . . . and after that I go out and party with them. The next day I'm babysitting one of their kids . . . I'm meeting up with one of them for lunch." Kimberly concluded by saying this dynamic has helped her grow as a person: "It's helped me grow a lot as a person to understand how a competitive sport works and how you can beat someone up on the track and go be their best friend 20 minutes later."

A number of women, whether new to female friendships or not, were pleasantly surprised by how supportive their leagues were. A few used the term *catty* to describe female dynamics in general and used *catty* to contrast their derby experience. For example, Helena described her league as "super supportive" and "tight-knit." She then said: "Women can sometimes be pretty catty when they're together, and I didn't see that with these ladies. It was just a different experience than anything I had ever had." Kimberly believes derby has made her nicer, compared to her days playing rugby:

> I didn't realize with rugby just how CATTY I could be with other girls, how MEAN I could be with other girls . . . And now I would NEVER say [something awful] about someone, even someone on another team, I would never be that catty. So, I think derby has made me a nicer person.

Though she did not use the word *catty*, Emma was surprised by how nicely everyone treats each other, given how jealous women can be with each other: "What I find surprising is how outgoing and chatty and nice the women are with each other. Because I think a lot of women, myself included, sometimes get that thing where you get jealous of other women." She explained that the sport could be a natural recipe for rivalries, instead she finds that the attitude is more inclusive: "It surprises me that people don't really have that [rivalry]. They're not, like, 'Oh, you're from that team and I'm from this team.' They're like, 'We're all derby and we're all friends!' (laughs) So I think that's pretty cool."

This "We're all derby and we're all friends" outlook extends to international skaters as well. Many women mentioned a derby network that connects people around the world. If a skater is traveling, she can contact the local team and not only be a guest skater at a practice, but likely will find people willing to host her: "People you had never met in your entire life and they're like, 'I'm coming to town and I want to skate with you.' Usually you take really good care of them. Just because they're part of that derby family. I've never seen this type of a community before and it's huge."

Julie posted on Facebook that she was heading to New York and someone immediately offered her a couch. As Julie put it: "(laughs) You can be awful at roller derby and people will still let you sleep on their couch." Suzy explained the network:

> I can go to any city in the US and most cities abroad and just look online and find a team and just ask anything like . . . "I'm traveling I need a place to stay, does anyone have an extra bed or couch that I could sleep on?" . . . It's a really cool honor system with derby where we're all in the same network. And we all dedicate so much of our lives and sacrifice so much to play the sport that we love that's still pretty underground.

Participants not only appreciated the reach of the derby network; they loved the diversity of the women involved, in terms of sexual orientation, income level, jobs and careers, age, and family/relationship status.

The great equalizer

Rae told me how she sees derby as a "great equalizer" because of the vast array of women she interacts with at derby:

> It's given me a lot of wonderful friends who I would've never met because like I said, I'm a hairstylist, I do graphic design on the side, I have friends that are doctors, but I probably would've never met friends that are geologists and engineers. There's every walk of life and that's the great thing. It's the great equalizer when we're out on the track.

Basma likewise recalled a number of professions represented in her league:

> I think the one thing that surprised me the most was the diversity of the women who were a part of derby . . . There's a lady who used to be one of those skiers that jump in the air and do all the tricks and stuff like that. There's a scientist and . . . young women, older women, divorced women, married women, just everybody that it brings together.

Basma added that her league feels more like a warm, encouraging family: "There's not a bunch of judgment . . . I think it's more of like a family than it is a league and people just are warm to each other and caring for each other."

Eliza acknowledged that a variety of jobs and careers are represented in derby, but she found age to be wide-ranging as well. At 36, she finds herself in the "upper echelon" of ages in her league. However, she finds this disparity in ages to be a positive aspect:

> You find yourself in social situations that you would not inherently find yourself in. I would probably not be hanging out with some of these girls because of their age . . . [or] because they're in different professions . . . or they live in a totally different area than I would ever visit, or they have just a lot of varying interests.

In contrast, when Julie began derby at 21, she was one of the youngest skaters in her league. She found the age differences to be helpful as her teammates encouraged her to return to school:

> Just being friends with all these [older] people really helped. I actually went back to school after starting roller derby just 'cause I had all these good influences and people saying, "Oh you can still do this, don't give up on school just cause it seems really stupid. It will eventually not be stupid."

Julie added that, because of their positive influence, she cannot picture what her life would look like without having met her teammates: "They're such fantastic people. I just can't imagine my life at this point without meeting some of them. Just because our social circles would have never hit each other otherwise."

Sarah described her league as representing "every walk of life" and as a result, "acceptance is really high":

> I love that it's everyone from every walk of life, every background you can image, every color and creed. And that was something that surprised me. I didn't expect really religious girls to play derby because it is so alternative and there's so many tattoos and piercing and parties and the beer. It's kind of like boys playing football and having frat parties, except it's the girls' style.

Lynn, a college professor, likes that derby challenges her assumptions about people's politics and religion, which is different from her experience at work: "I can pretty much know in general where [colleagues are] going to sit on the political line, the religion line, and this has been a good reminder that I can't make that assumption about everyone (laughs)."

Madeline refers to the diversity more in terms of personalities than other demographic differences:

> Some people in derby are very strange. Some people are just average people who want to do something new. Some people are ex-athletes or have had an athletic background. Some people are housewives or stay at home mums. You have just a bunch of different personalities.

Audra provided a nice summary for participants' sentiments on the supportiveness of the community as being a major draw to remaining in the sport despite the hurdles:

> I think just a lot of it is the really amazing community of women. It's just such strong awesome women who play. That's just wonderful and I love it. It's just this space where regardless of people's backgrounds or what their world views are, a lot of them are just really amazing women who think that women can kick ass. It's just such a supportive environment.

In short, women cited numerous benefits of derby, including health, therapeutic, and social benefits. Women loved being a part of a diverse community, where they can build female friendships in adulthood.

A like-minded, supportive community

Another benefit the women gained from derby is access to a like-minded, supportive community. Some mentioned being thankful for a sports community that provides them with a healthy hobby. Others were proud to be connected to a charitable and civically-minded organization.

Emma described what the derby community means to her:

> It is a safe space where people can truly be themselves . . . It is being included in something that maybe was previously seen to be out of reach for them, and that is to be included in a sport, to not be judged for anything, and to participate in whatever level you can participate in, in a sport where everybody is celebrated for what makes them special.

Brooke noted the sympathetic, "like-minded" nature of her derby community:

> When you're at home, you've got responsibilities, to your children and to your husband, and you've got work and everything else. When

you go to derby, you have a bunch of females with you. You have a bunch of women that you're working out with and you're supporting, and you're, you know, you're getting a lot of love from them and, you know, feeling that.

Audra shared that building a supportive community can be hard as an adult: "As an adult once you leave college it can be really hard to get that sense of community, you know, being around really amazing people who are like positive and uplifting and who are there for you." Lucy agreed that it is difficult to build friendships post-college:

> As an adult it was an effective way to make friends. Even the most outgoing people as adults find it hard to make new friends. It's not what you do. It's much more difficult. The fact that it finally allowed me to have this outlet where in a very natural way I was able to make new friends – just like you did when you were a kid . . . You don't get that once you're out of college.

When participants speak of derby expanding not only their social life but their circle of close friends, I am reminded of the idea of "refrigerator rights," or those people in your life who have permission to raid your fridge without asking. Miller and Sparks (2015) argued that the number of people in our lives with refrigerator rights is decreasing due to a variety of factors, including moving away from our extended families, our culture of individualism, and increased use of media. Derby helps combat this trend by bringing together compatible yet unrelated women and bonding them together through this physical sport. While one benefit of derby is access to the international derby network, derby clearly also provides impactful, close, and supportive relationships at a time in many adults' lives, and at a time in our society, that is increasingly isolating.

Some of the women appreciate derby for its focus on strengthening community through charitable giving and volunteering. Maya cited the "rewarding feeling" she gets by being a part of positive, contributing organization: "It's definitely one of the few organizations that's so positive in your own life and for others, and everybody feels good when they're contributing to something and helping other people rather than helping yourself. It's a very rewarding feeling." Rae expressed how giving her league is, including helping her raise $10,000 for the Multiple Sclerosis Society: "The derby community is by far one of the most giving and supportive communities I've ever known. I was able to raise over $10,000 for the MS Society just because of my derby family." She mentioned a skater in another league who had a spinal fracture and needed major surgery. Unfortunately, under their insurance, the skater is responsible for the first $5,000. Rae said: "Overnight the derby community was able to raise $5,000 to pay for her surgery . . . I think that's a big part of it too, the reason why it continues to grow. That community and that sense of family."

Eliza sees derby's commitment to charitable giving as admirable: "I have always tried to be relatively civic-minded. So I have volunteered in the past prior to derby. But the fact that derby prioritizes charitable giving, I think, is really admirable . . . It makes me respect derby organizations more." Lucy likewise finds positive elements in the nonprofit nature of derby: "Especially being a part of orchestrating how things go, not just as a successful business but as a nonprofit organization that does give back to the community, that's very meaningful to me." She elaborated that she is unable to compete at the highest level but is still able to derive benefits from her community: "I'm not on the all-star team for a variety of reasons . . . Even so, I can find this fulfilling. I don't have to be the top competitor and I can still be fulfilled by my participation in a non-athletic way." Sarah similarly highlighted the volunteer nature of her particular community – that many people contribute in non-athletic ways: "One of the great things about roller derby being all volunteers. Nobody gets paid, even the coaches. Everyone in derby is a volunteer. They're there because they want to be there." Nearly everyone admitted they would likely remain in derby long after they "hung up their skates" because of the community. Bridgett is just one example:

> Derby is such a physical sport that eventually your body wears out. But there's so many things that you can do in roller derby without having to play but you can still put a major impact on the sport . . . I want to forever be in this group of girls because they're so awesome and the sport is so amazing. Unless something, like, super-drastic happens, I don't see myself leaving derby.

Rae summarizes the impact of community on those involved: "Sometimes you turn on the news and it's just so negative all of the time and [derby] restores your faith in humanity because there are so many different facets in derby where it's the community, it's the athleticism. All of that combined is mind blowing."

This chapter answered the question posed by Chapter 2: if derby is so expensive, requiring a large time commitment, and serious injuries are common, why do women play? I asked participants that question and they recited numerous benefits. Women stick with derby because of the physical and mental health benefits, improved self-confidence and body image, as well as the benefits to having a "cathartic" outlet for their aggression.

Finally, women shared that derby has given them an expanded social circle that includes close, supportive female friendships. Sadly, a few participants explained these supportive female friendships is a new experience for them. Next, I devote Chapter 4 to an interesting – and similarly beneficial – aspect of roller derby, that of the "derby persona," at times referred to as an alter ego.

Reference

Miller, W. & Sparks, G.G. (2015). *Refrigerator rights: Creating connections and restoring relationships* (2nd ed.). Amherst, MA: White River Press.

4 The role of the alter ego/derby persona

The previous chapter discussed the myriad ways participants benefitted from roller derby. This chapter continues by discussing another element of roller derby that many of the women say they benefitted from: the derby persona, at times referred to as their alter ego. As mentioned in Chapter 1, the majority of players skate under aliases, or pseudonyms. One of the Frequently Asked Questions on the Women's Flat Track Derby Association, WFTDA, web site describes the derby persona as:

> Skaters are "normal" during the day. We work, we're moms, students, etc. Roller derby is our escape from day-to-day life and our opportunity to embrace a tougher, edgier side of ourselves. When you step into the rink, your derby alter ego takes over.
>
> (WFTDA, 2016)

Though the WFTDA's own web site describes the derby persona as a completely different side of them (i.e., a true alter ego), the reality is that for many of the women in this study, their derby name is merely a persona and not a true alter ego. One reason I faced so much difficulty finding interview subjects is because many women are tired of roller derby articles focusing on the alter ego aspect at the expense of acknowledging other factors, like the growth of the sport, the athleticism of is players, or how derby gives back to their communities. In addition, participants noted that as the sport grows in popularity, becoming mainstreamed, some "theatrical" aspects such as playing in tutus and fishnet stockings and the alter ego seem to be phasing out.

I bear this shift in mind as I wrote this chapter, seeking not to alienate any derby athletes who might see "alter ego" in the Table of Contents and sigh at another one-dimensional portrayal or even dismiss this study outright. Lucy described this tiresome coverage:

> [It's always] art teacher by day, cruiser by night. It's an important part of the history of the culture. I don't run away from it but it's just one

very interesting, not necessarily shallow, but one dimension. There's a lot of other depth to [derby] in other ways. That's what makes it I think discouraging to get just that kind of coverage.

Emma concurred:

> You know, people come out to interview us all the time, but yeah, it is kind of like the same story and each journalist thinks – I know you're not a journalist – but each journalist thinks "I really have this great angle" and it's like "We've read this story a thousand times." (laughs)

Therefore, my goal of this chapter is to accurately describe how derby names work while realistically depicting the spectrum of my participants: some experience a true alter ego on one end of the spectrum, while others adamantly posit that their derby name is nothing more than a fun name on the other. In the middle of this spectrum lie most of my participants, women whose personas – not alter egos – confer certain benefits, such as amplifying existing parts of their personality or facilitating the emergence of others. Finally, a few women mentioned the privacy the derby persona affords them in both: (a) their personal life with fans and (b) their professional life with coworkers and employers.

Before examining the multitude of ways the women enjoy skating under aliases, I outline what the derby names are and how women choose them. Please note that due to the confidentiality I promised participants, I am unable to share the imaginative and often hilarious derby names of my participants. Therefore, as illustrative examples, I selected names from two online registries: *Two Evils* and *Derby Roll Call*. *Two Evils* is much older than the more recent *Derby Roll Call*. For that reason, I pull most of the sample names from *Two Evils*.

A rite of passage

After the women reach a particular stage in the tryout process, they are able to create and register a name. Participants varied in how their league chose when a woman could pick a name. A few said they had been skating for 1–2 months before getting a name, another said she had to wait six months. Though there seemed to be variations across the various leagues, the consensus was that you do not simply get to choose a name on the first day you show up. Rather, getting a derby name is a "rite of passage."

Skaters are responsible for picking their own name and they typically, though not always, choose two names, a first and last name, that often results in a pun or double entendre. The names are often creative, funny, intimidating, or sexy, or some combination of those adjectives. For example, a woman might choose the name *Donna Matrix, Venus Thigh Trap,* or *Buzz Tightrear.* Some of the names incorporate existing common female names, such as *Amanda* (A man to . . .) or *Anita* (I need to . . .) or *Megan* (Making . . .), in order to create a pun. Sometimes the women really are named Amanda, Anita, and Megan, and sometimes not. Some names coalesce around a particular verb, for examples, there are many names that are variations of "Rip her", e.g., *Rippa Heartout* and *Ripper Intwo.* According to participants, after creating their name, they then tend to be called a shortened version of that name. For example, Claire D. Way would likely just be called Claire and Barbitchuit would likely be called Barb.

Registering your name

Once a woman selects a name, she can head to the *Derby Roll Call* web site to register her name. Before *Derby Roll Call,* women would use the web site *Two Evils* to register their names. The idea behind registering one's name is to prevent overlap. However, roller derby has spread so far around the world that would be impossible to track every name. To illustrate the difficulty in creating a unique name, the *Two Evils* Registry registered 40,542 names between 2004–2014, and as of March 2018, Derby Roll call has over 33,000 names. *Derby Roll Call* acknowledges the inevitability of duplication on their site:

> Given how many people are finding out about derby every single day, it's inevitable two people will come up with the same name at the same

Table 4.1 Sample Names Taken from *Two Evils* Derby Registry. Note the variety of funny, violent, and sexy names, the use of puns, how women's names are incorporated into the pun, as well as how a phrase like *Rip Her* can be taken in a few directions.

Amanda Spank	BareLeigh Legal	Claire D. Way	Donna Matrix	Second Hand Smoke
Amandatory Beating	Bee A. Frayed	Racer McChaser	Venus Thigh Trap	Rippa Heartout
American Just Ass	Bomb Jovi	Suzy Hotrod	Buzz Tightrear	Rippa NewOne
Megan M. Hurt	Shenita Stretcher	Bio-diesel	Diet Choke	Ripper A. Part
Megan M. Bleed	Tannibel Lector	Snot Rocket Science	Diet Spite	Ripper Intwo
Barbitchuit	Frida Beater	Sew Crafty	Cruella E. Vil	Ripper Limbsoff

time. Who are we to decide who got there first? The site's approach is to accept this duplication and try to inform everyone about the situation.

(Derby Roll Call, 2018)

"A lot of thought, blood, sweat, and tears"

The women shared how choosing a name is both a rite of passage and pressure-filled. Madeline said: "Getting your roller derby name is a pretty big thing. It's like a rite of passage. You were here long enough, now you get to get your cool kick-ass derby name." Unfortunately for Alexis, she doesn't like her real name, so she felt pressure to think of a name before people resorted to only using her real name: "If you don't come up with a derby name soon enough people just call you by your real name, so it sticks with you and it's just solidified in their head (laughs)." Andrea also felt pressure: "I felt a little pressure at first because everybody was choosing their names." She added: "and it's hard to come up with a name. You go to different sites, you put different things together, try to fit your personality, something that speaks to who you are." Brooke described the process of getting a name in her league:

> It's a really big thing to be able to get your roller derby name. We have new recruits who come into our league and they have to skate with their real name for a while and then when they become a league member, they're allowed to officially register their name.

Like others, she mentioned the online registries and said: "Everything's registered. It's a really big deal. It's a coming of age for derby I guess to get that privilege to skate with a derby name." It is such a big deal that one woman would not tell me her derby name. She was a few days away from being able to officially register it and did not want it stolen. She said:

> I'm not telling because so many women have stories of their names being stolen before they're able to put it in. So yeah it's kind of this big secret no one talks about . . . people do suffer when they have their name stolen.

She did not mean that names were stolen within the same league, "but you know they tell people and they put it on Facebook or someone's stalking it, then someone else thought oh that's a great name . . . and all of a sudden it's gone. Sorry." To summarize the stress and pressure to pick a "good" derby name, Sophia said: "There's a lot of thought and blood, sweat, and tears that goes into picking a roller derby name."

"What's in a name?"

I also asked the women how they created their name and received a variety of responses. Again, to protect the confidentiality of participants, I can only describe their names vaguely. Two of the women based their name around nicknames they have had for years. Bridgett chose her name in tribute to her late aunt, who was sporty and who "would have loved derby," by using her old AOL username: "And so I kind of took using her name as, like, a memorial of her." Tina selected a combination of her two favorite superheroes, and because she sees herself as big and tough on the inside, though she is smaller in stature: "And the fact that I'm like this little tiny person and in my head I'm like you know tough, like tough girl (laughs) so I thought it was kind of fitting all around." Julie said: "I wanted something that sort of suited my personality a little bit, and I'm very outspoken, and eventually, at some point or another, I'm probably going to tick off somebody that knows me by being outspoken," Similarly, Audra chose her name based off of her playing style: "My favorite part of derby is getting to knock the crap out of people and I've gotten a reputation among the newer players for having really hard hits and being able to knock the crap out of people so it's fitting for me."

Maude chose her name for the opposite reason; she is not intimidating at all. Her name pays tribute to her half-Japanese heritage but also to her personality:

> I like it because it's the least intimidating name you really hear (laughs). It's just, like, "HELLO!" (laughs) . . . I don't like to be intimidating like that. I'm not – I don't paint my face black and get all scary. I just want to play really hard and, like, go drink a beer.

Like Maude, Basma wanted to pay tribute to her heritage in at least part of her name: "My heritage is Aztec and Mexican . . . So I wanted to make sure that I incorporated that in my name, and . . . the [second part of her name] kinda just came because everyone's always tellin' me how crazy I am."

Many of the women selected their alias based on interests or hobbies, such as reading, history, science, soccer, the Beatles, or a specific television show or movie. For example, Ruth said she picked her name to match her "old-fashioned sensibility": "I have an old-fashioned sensibility I guess. I like vintage and retro and things from the past. My husband teases that I want rotary phones instead of the 21st century and there's a lot romance in that to me." One scientist chose her name based on the type of fish she studies while another player picked her name based on a Beatles song.

Eliza wanted to pick a clever name and liked reading fairy tales growing up. She found an old, little-known fairy tale where the princess is the heroine who rescues the prince and "I think that kind of epitomizes roller derby in the fact that it's, you know, empowering women and strength and, you know, aggression? Well, maybe not aggression, but assertiveness and independence, and I thought that was great." A bonus for Eliza is that the fairy tale works as a double entendre: it sounds a bit dirty and violent, but in reality is the actual name of a little-known European fairy tale. She continued: "I really like the name, and I like the story behind it, so that makes it great so that when children come up to me in a parade and ask me why I picked the name [redacted], I have a story for them." She noted that it is something she can tell the parents at the parades, as well: "So I got my bases covered."

Andrea likewise wanted to create a name that was "clean, you know, for my children . . . just to be classy." A friend suggested a name that blended her name and a word that means "risk-taker" and "not fearful and not afraid." The suggestion fit her because she says of herself: "Personality-wise, I've always been someone who says, 'Okay, let's do it, let's try it and let's get good at it.'"

Another mother, Joanna, wanted a name that would be appropriate if her then-young children said it aloud at school:

> I'd thrown around a bunch of names, and like my favorite liquid to drink is whisky, so everybody was like 'oh you really should have something with whisky in it . . . I'm thinking, well I want something that they can say at school, so I don't want anything profane in it.'

One woman went the opposite route and chose a name that would evoke war to keep people thinking about Canadian soldiers dying:

> So I sort of picked the name because it was sort of frustrating from an anti-war activist perspective that people weren't really thinking about the way, they weren't talking about it except when there was news that more Canadians came home in body bags.

She continued:

> People don't want to think about or prefer not to think about or are uncomfortable to talk about, you know, real violence, and yet enjoy the

idea of an all-girls full-contact sport, which is violent (laughs). So yeah, I guess I picked the name because I thought that it would be shocking.

Another woman chose her name because her sister, who joined roller derby first, thought it would be nice to have matching names: "She brought up the idea that there's not a lot of sister or mother/daughters or cousins or anybody that she knew that shared names and it was something unique for the two of us."

Many players create emails and social media pages using just their derby names. This means that when willing participants would email me, my inbox was filled with head turning email addresses, using names such as *Maniac* or *Psycho*. In one exchange with an interviewee, Patrice, I mentioned how I was unsure of the proper protocol for addressing emails (i.e., how to greet someone named *Shaneeda Spankin*, or whether to say, "*Hello, are you Psycho?*" when meeting the interviewee at a coffee shop, for example). Patrice replied that it is even more complicated than that: "Not only that but what's the nickname . . . and so you have to learn the full derby name, you have to learn the [shortened] derby name then you have to figure out who the heck they are in real life." One woman, Emma, also told me that, in her league at least, most people do not know someone's real name, and if you do, that means you are more than a teammate, you are a closer friend:

> It sometimes becomes that you only know somebody's real name if you become better friends with them. And within some leagues, at least mine, if you know somebody's real name and refer to them as their real name, that means you're probably a closer friend to them.

The rules and customs behind the names may differ across leagues, but one common function of the names is that they serve as a sort of status symbol for the skaters who earned them.

The role of the derby persona/alter ego

I asked the women to describe their derby persona or how it has impacted their life and their answers represented a spectrum, from "*My New Year's resolution is to be more like [derby name]*" to "*It's just a name*," with "*It's just like that idealized version of me*" in the middle. I begin with those women who view their persona as a true alter ego, or separate selves (Kihlstrom, 2010), that they "become" while in the arena.

Rae, who said, "I found myself playing derby," really "liked the idea of having an alter ego and I wanted the whole story behind it." She told me that her alter ego has become a bigger part of her to the extent that she was working on changing her name legally to the first part of her derby name: "It's just become a bigger part of me, my derby name . . . so officially I'm working on trying to change my name to [derby name]. Everybody knows me by that, so it's just taken over my life in that aspect too."

Joanna referred to her alter ego as her "second being," and said:

> When I put skates on though, I'm not this mild mannered, let's go hang out, let's go sledding, go to work and be nice to customers. I want to get on the track, and my objective is to stop everyone that I can stop, and knock anyone down I can knock down!

Joanna, who has her own company requiring daily customer interaction, noted that having roller derby and her alter ego as an outlet helps her deal with customers. She added, "Some people that have known me for a lot of years have said that I'm a much nicer person since I started playing roller derby!"

Natalie similarly feels more aggressive on the rink because of her alter ego. She said:

> If I see the girl on the opposite team is having a hard time, in my heart, as a good person, I want to let up on her and just be like, "Just go ahead babe, your face is bleeding and you're crying and I know you can't take another hit from me, so just go ahead," but the competitive athlete me is like "Just keep hitting her."

I asked her if this degree of aggression was different from her extensive history with other contact sports and she answered: "Right, I wouldn't have had that boldness in basketball. It is like an alter ego. It is like, 'I'm fucking [derby name], shut the fuck up, get out of my way, I'm going to kill you, I'm going to roll over you.'"

Meagan, whose name references a famous fictional serial killer, said that she chose her name specifically to help her "break out of my shell." She said: "I think picking a name that reflects one of, personally I think, one of the best movie films of all time, I think it kind of puts an edge then." She noted that the name helps get her ready to play: "It helped me get into the character and I definitely think when I play that I almost have a split personality. I feel like I'm (pause) a lot more aggressive and it's definitely a different mindset for me." She then told me she wears the fictional serial killer's famous mask during the introductions at bouts. She said:

> People look at me and their like, "Oh my god, like who is this crazy?" and I'm like, "Don't mess with ME." (laughs) It's a lot of fun like playing up that character because I mean (pause) they only see what I'm like on the track so if they think that I'm scary then that's OK, it's an advantage. (laughs)

For Meagan, the mask helps convey a façade of toughness that helps during competition.

When I asked Joanna, who had previously made clear that her derby persona is an actual alter ego, what the relationship between Joanna and her alter ego is, she responded,

> They get along! They kind of fight sometimes, because one wants me more aggressive, and then at home, Joanna is like, no no no, you have to be responsible! Whereas Vixen is a little more aggressive, and wants to just go and do whatever she wants to do!

Knowing she had older children, I asked what her children thought of her alter ego, she said, "I get the 'derby drama.' It's what they usually call it. 'Mom, stop with the derby drama.'" I then asked Joanna what that means, and she said:

> It basically means stop being my alter ego! Just be my mom, just be my mom. You don't have to be the drill sergeant. And I train [her daughter, who skates in junior derby] too, so I run a practice, and they call me the drill sergeant, because when the skates are on, I'm strict.

While a small handful of women see their derby self as a distinct alter ego, Rae's alter ego has blurred with her "real identity," or, as she says, they have "become one." As Rae said,

> That's the thing. It was my alter ego, but now that alter ego and my true self have become one I guess. I grew as a person since I've been playing and like I said, I've become more confident. It's just exuded that and it helped me just grow my person and now that's who I am.

Clearly, for the women experiencing a true alter ego, embracing this side of derby has imparted meaningful benefits.

"An idealized version of me"

While the "librarian by day, roller girl by night" juxtaposition of alter egos fascinates many outsiders, including journalists, in reality, most of my participants view their derby name as more of a fun persona than a dual personality. These women exist in the middle ground of the alter ego continuum of my participants. This group of women view their derby name as more of a persona, one that confers benefits ranging from augmenting existing personality traits to facilitating the emergence of others. For example, Alexis said of her derby persona,

> I want to be that strong, confident woman who is sure of herself and who can take criticism well and be a leader and that kind of stuff . . . So, it's not like I'm mean or tough or badass persona, it's just like that idealized version of me.

Eliza provided a similar answer: "I feel like a more empowered me, and I feel like a more exaggerated me." Eliza added that because she is woman working in IT, she is already in a "kind of gender-breaking role . . . and as a result of that, I work with all men and I have to be more aggressive, be more assertive, be more confident about my skills and my capabilities when I present myself in business."

Like Eliza's version of an "empowered" and "exaggerated" version of herself, Ruth said that her alter ego turns up her personality: "Roller derby and having an alter ego has brought out or let me be a little bit louder in my regular personality." Rather than seeing her persona as someone who gets "into more shenanigans" than her real self, she views her alter ego as giving her a bit of freedom: "I think that having an alter ego lets you have some sort of freedom." She qualifies her view by saying "some sort of freedom" because she does not feel constrained in her everyday life in the way other skaters might feel. She said, "[I don't] feel constrained in my everyday life in a way that having [derby name] as an alter ego frees me." In other words, she has less of an alter ego because she has less of a need for one. Instead, for Ruth, derby helped draw out existing parts of her character: "Roller derby in general has made me more aware of things that were already a part of my character."

Lucy also does not feel the need to cultivate another personality in order to become more aggressive, and like Ruth, she attributes this to the freedom she feels in her non-derby life:

> My derby name is not going to be a more aggressive, scary, hostile, intimidating one – it's very neutral. I don't need that but maybe some

people do. Maybe in order to embrace that side of themselves, they need the alternate identity. Or maybe because in their personal lives or professionally it makes a little bit more sense to keep those things separate.

In contrast to these perspectives, Kimberly told me how she is developing *into* the alias that she created:

> I find that there are things that as I sort of developed into derby and into the alias that I sort of created with this name, like this whole personality that goes with it, I'm finding a side of my personality coming out that I didn't know I HAD. I'm more like outgoing, an outrageous side that I didn't think I had.

I probed this response by asking if she sees this personality in her non-derby life and she laughed and responded yes, and that she recently dyed her hair for the first time and got a tattoo: "I got a tattoo of course because as soon as you start playing derby it seems you end up getting a tattoo. Yeah, little things like that." However, she emphasized that aspects of her personality have changed as well.

> I mean NOT just, NOT just physical stuff too there's aspects of my personality – I'm more, I'm single right now and I'm not as afraid to go out and just like I recently just like gave a guy my number which is something I never would have done.

She attributes this confidence to derby:

> But I think I have all this confidence built up from all the success I've been having at derby so it was kind of like you know, "He'll give me a call if he wants to, or if he doesn't it doesn't matter because I'm [derby name]" so who cares. I'm awesome all on my own.

Maura likewise mentioned the courage she gains from her persona. Whereas many derby personas are loud and in-your-face, she described hers as "pretty chill, stays pretty calm." When I asked her if that is how she would describe her own personality, she replied, "I am not as calm and collected as I would like to be in my everyday life. There have definitely been days where I have wanted to take on my skater personality for some things in my everyday life." I asked her for an example and she mentioned having developed test anxiety since beginning a graduate program:

> So whenever we had written exams or anything like that, it was just a horrible experience for me, and I've always been, like, "I wish I could

just wear skates to class" (laughs). Wear my helmet or something so I just feel a little more at ease.

Though a peculiar site to imagine, Maura is describing the very real sense of strength she derives from this identity. Similarly, Julie gains courage from her derby persona, while noting it is not a separate person. She said, it is *not* like,

> I'm one person here and one person somewhere else, but it's definitely like, when we go out and do like a derby promotion thing, [persona] is definitely much more extroverted than Julie so you can go talk to strangers and that's okay. (laughs)

Just a name

After sharing stories of women who have an alter ego and women who describe more of a helpful and fun persona, I want to include those women who were very clear that they see no distinction between their real and derby self.

Brooke was clear she sees no deviation in her derby and real self: "I don't think I deviate at all. I think I'm very much the same person. I know a lot of people will tell you they become this totally different person when they get on the track, and I don't think I do at all." She shared her attitude during competition, but like many athletes in other sports, that is not necessarily tied to an alter ego: "I'm a serious person in real life, and I get on the track, and I put on my jammer face, and I'm skating, and . . . My persona gets carried over onto the track with me. I don't have an alter-ego really."

Shannon prefers to skate under a different name but retains her usual personality. Of the derby personas, she said, "I am the same person (laughs), so it doesn't really matter to me. I've never wanted to be known as my real name." She dislikes her real name because it sounds like a female body part and her derby name is a play on this name. Derby helped her reclaim a source of derision and teasing. She said she has finally "embraced the fact that I've been teased for so long because of my horrible last name, and why would I start that all over again? Putting that out there as my real name."

Julie told me that she sees the alter ego as fading out as it was more popular when derby resurfaced. Now, she said,

> I think of myself more as just an athlete who has this name (laughs). For me there's no difference between [given name] and [derby name]. I don't know if everybody would say that, but [for me] That's the same person, there's just not much of a difference.

Lynn agrees that for her, her derby persona is just a different name: "I don't really act any differently, and I would say that's true for most of the girls on my team." She and a few others mentioned this trend toward skating under their real names as an attempt to "be taken seriously, because it IS a serious sport." She said of some leagues: "Some of the leagues want to differentiate from the old roller derby that used to be on TV where you had these names, these personas, and it was kind of like WWE, right, where there's a lot of fake things." However, despite this move, Lynn likes skating under a different name, though she maintains the same personality: "So people are starting to skate under their real names. I kind of like having a different name, but I don't have really a different personality, because I kind of like mine (laughs)."

Challenging derby's legitimacy?

A few of the women discussed the debate over phasing out derby names. The general consensus was that, though not all the women reported any differences between their real self and their derby self, they love skating under a different name. They acknowledge that the debate stems from a desire to be taken more seriously and to distance the current sport from the fake fighting from decades ago. However, the women relish the uniqueness the names give their sport. Eliza said, "I am not a fan of trying to sterilize the sport. You know, make everything monochromatic, make everything happy and nice . . . I like the idea that we can have crazy derby names, but I don't know. Time will tell." When I asked Audra if she likes skating under a different name, she said, "I do. I enjoy it. I mean I can understand why certain leagues are moving away from that." She acknowledges the debate when she says: "I think a lot of that is because it used to have this history of not being taken seriously and in the past I think it was something silly that people watched on television and I think it's like women want the sport to be taken seriously." Yet at the same time, she hopes that derby can retain what she calls the "theatricality" and the "spectacle" because it helps sell tickets:

> To be frank too, I think having that element helps us to sell tickets to bouts and stuff because it's the sort of larger than life, the ridiculous outfits and the names and personas and I think it sort of really gets people invested in the game.

Of the idea that people want to drop derby names in order to gain legitimacy, Maude thinks derby already is a legitimate sport: "I think it's a legitimate sport. I think it's completely a legitimate sport. I don't know what kind of recognition people are waiting for."

Mary Ellen enjoys the celebrity behind the names as an escape from her day-to-day identity as a coworker and soccer mom. Of skating under a derby name, she said: "I love it. Absolutely love it." I then asked her if there was any particular reason why and she replied that skating under her own name is "nothing special." She continued:

> You say "Mary Ellen" and people think "Oh our database administrator" or "the mom who brings Daniel to soccer practice," but skating out there and they see the [derby name] on my back or they hear the announcer saying [my derby name], there's a sense of "Oh my god, I know her, I know somebody famous."

She continued, "It's a very different attitude using the derby name. Nobody wants a signature or an autograph from Mary Ellen, but there are lots of people who will come up afterwards and 'Oh, can I have your autograph?'"

In addition to liking the names because of the uniqueness it adds to the sport, some of the women are now known by different names, and they appreciate that change to their life. Julie explained that she likes having a name that she chose herself:

> I love the nickname aspect of it so. It always bums me out when people are like, "Oh play under your real names and blah blah blah," and I'm like, "Oh, I've had that name forever like this is the name I got to pick myself."

Natalie agreed: "I love it [playing under a name] . . . Even football players are called the 'dump truck' or the 'refrigerator.' It's cool."

Though Emma does not have an alter ego, she largely now goes by the first word in her derby name (a word similar to Smash): "I am the same person for sure, but [Smash] is my name now (laughs). You know? Like half of my friends, maybe more than half of them, refer to me by that name." She explained how the derby names in effect become a person's name because people would not know how to contact you because they do not know your real name – unless you are a close derby friend:

> I guess it is a nickname, but it is my name . . . It sometimes becomes that you only know somebody's real name if you become better friends with them. And within some leagues, at least mine, if you know somebody's real name and refer to them as their real name, that means you're probably a closer friend to them . . . if I didn't have my derby name on my Facebook, for instance, half of the people wouldn't know what my

name was to invite me to events, and they wouldn't know what my name was to tag me in pictures.

Others love the name because they worked really hard for it. Sarah loves it because she worked hard to earn her name:

> It's really fun to have your derby name and it takes you six months in my league to earn it. So you work really hard to get your derby name and you have to meet all these commitments and skill levels and everything to earn your name.

At the same time, Sarah would skate under her real name if she got to keep playing: "But for me I could really go either way. I just love this derby." Sandra similarly sees her name as a badge of honor: "Yeah. I enjoy it. I worked hard to get it, and it's kind of funny. I think if anything, it just makes me smile a little. I enjoy that it kind of lifts some of the seriousness away." Sandra also believes that derby names do not dilute the legitimacy of the sport:

> I think people need to understand that the reason we have these names is because we've dedicated a large amount of time to this sport and because of that we have something to show for it that you can see. I think that's very important. I think that distinction is something that people don't get in other sports. It's very nice to know that all these women worked that hard to get to this level. If anything, I think that's what it really brings to the sport. I don't think it dumbs it down any less . . . I don't know why there are people who think it dumbs it down. I just don't agree with that on any level. You look at boxers, or MMA fighters. They all have nicknames. To me I just look at it like a nickname. I'm okay with keeping it.

Finally, Alexis likes playing under a name as it gives her courage to be a jammer: "that's part of what helps me go out there and be a jammer and be someone who takes responsibility or whatever and (pause) and I don't know (laughs)." Though earlier Alexis stated that her derby persona was more of an "idealized version of me," she "jokes" about the inability to play derby without a persona:

> I've actually joked that you know, if it ever comes to people having to play under their real names, I would strongly consider legally changing my actual name to [Derby Name]. I don't have a problem being [Derby Name] in my regular life, I have a problem being Alexis in derby. (laughs)

Thus, to many participants, the derby persona may not be an alter ego, but it is certainly more than a name. A derby name is a badge of honor and a fun, creative way of establishing in-group status within the sport.

Cloak of anonymity

Another reason the women preferred to play under an alias is the privacy it affords them. Julie said the names help protect the women from aggressive fans:

> It also gives you just a little bit of anonymity. I'm not saying that fans are crazy (laughs) by any means, but derby gives people very up-close access to skaters. So your fans are standing on the side of the track, they're giving you high-fives as you skate by, they start to feel really connected to you.

She added that the name helps her feel safer: "And I think having that pseudonym makes us feel just a little bit (pause) safer, maybe. I don't know, at least that's how I feel." The way she paused before choosing the word *safer* made me think that she was being careful not to say anything too negative about the enthusiastic fans. Madeline agreed: "It keeps your identity separate from your legal identity." She said she does not have to worry about "stalkers" because:

> If [someone] comes up and asks me my name, I'll say [my derby name] and they'll be like "Well, what's your *name*," . . . and I'm like "It's [derby name]" . . . It kind of kills their "Oh, you're not going to tell me your name," and I'm like "Nope. Not unless I have a real big reason to."

Madeline likened this anonymity to celebrities: "It's like a lot of celebrities. They have stage names and real names. Its protection and something that's cool. It serves multiple purposes." Helena concurred that this anonymity also helps on social media, where she goes by her derby name and not her legal name: "There were some people who were inappropriate, and then there were some people who were just playful about, you know, [my sexy derby persona], and you know, I would have these really bizarre interactions with people [on social media]." Natalie shared a positive but nevertheless interesting anecdote about social media and derby fame:

> I remember the first time I saw – I took a picture with a fan and they had tagged me in it and made it their profile picture, and I remember the feeling, because I was like "I don't know this person, that's amazing."

In addition to the anonymity their alias affords them when interacting with fans, they also benefit from the shield it provides their career. Kimberly mentioned that while her peers actually come to bouts, her supervisors do not know she plays roller derby. She is concerned about the damage to her professional identity if her two worlds collide, as she has been recognized because of posters and other promotions:

> All of my media stuff that I do online, I do it under my derby alias and I don't plan on crossing those two parts of my life, which is something I'm a little bit concerned about because I'm starting to get recognized now as [derby name]. (laughs)

She mentioned that she is a "TAD bit concerned" but hopes that her young age will help people "brush it off" without affecting her professional life. The reason she hopes her young age will foster a positive reception by her supervisors is because Kimberly plays with a woman in the same career path but ten years ahead of her and *she* is concerned what her older peers would think of her playing derby. Kimberly said of this teammate and colleague:

> We just had a photo shoot this past weekend and she was talking about how if her coworkers or if her supervisor saw those pictures, what would they think of her? So for her, having the derby alias has been very valuable because she's been able to keep that part of her life very separate from what is you know, a more professional part of her life.

For Shannon, who moved across the country to play for another derby league, she appreciated having the alias as she searched for jobs. She said she did not want a future employer to Google her and see:

> all these outrageous pictures of things that I'd been doing with derby over the years and that would be my overriding Internet search instead of, you know, my professional career and the name I've made for myself in that other world that I live in.

Though Shannon found a job where she eventually felt comfortable telling coworkers that she plays derby, she is not sure making her "alternative life-style" so visible would have helped her:

> Now that I've got this job at this super conservative place, and I mean, I am married to a woman, I play roller derby, which is a very out there

sport, you know, I live this alternative lifestyle and it doesn't need to be the first thing that they see, you know? (laughs)

She is not sure whether she "would have been hired or considered had this super conservative company – had they known every other aspect of me." To be clear, some women had no problem with their employers and coworkers knowing they played roller derby, though I perceive this has a lot to do with the type of industry they work in as well as the type of organization. Meagan, who works in advertising, said not only does it not impact her job, she would be proud to skate under her real name:

> It doesn't impact me in any way with my job. I work in advertising and everybody I work with knows that I play derby . . . If I had a jersey with my last name on it I would feel really PROUD.

Though Julie is not worried about her own "professional reputation," she understands how some women might be: "My work is well aware that I play derby, they think it's cool, they want to come to bouts. But other people, I think, who are in highly professional, visible roles sometimes really don't want to connect those two worlds. They want to be this professional person and this derby skater." Suzy also understands this concern but feels that as the sport progresses, maintaining their professional reputations will be less of a concern:

> I think it's less and less of a worry as time goes on (pause) because it's becoming more legitimate. I think as the reporting (pause) is more accurate of what, of the climate and what's actually going on in derby, I think that'll be less of a concern later.

In a time when managing one's online presence become imperative for career and safety reasons, derby aliases provide a cloak of anonymity that other hobbies or sports do not have. This anonymity allows women to safely explore their alter egos or personas and to experiment with different gender expressions.

"That's pretty cool"

Though many of the women were adamant that they do not have a separate, dual-personality type of alter ego, the overwhelming consensus of my participants is that they love skating under derby names. The women gained many benefits from playing under a derby persona, from finding the courage to play and interact with fans to providing anonymity as needed. Sophia, who emphasized that she does *not* have an alter ego, nevertheless had this to say about the world of derby, complete with the creative names and idealizing, sometimes freeing personas:

> It's kind of cool to have that separation of somebody that you are on a day-to-day basis with your job and at home, and then you go to roller derby and it's just this other world. That's pretty cool.

This chapter examined derby names and personas, including benefits conferred from playing under derby names. The next chapter explores derby personas as just one feature of a sport that overall, reveals much about current societies. In short, the next chapter tackles the overarching question behind my study: *Why derby? Why now?* By examining roller derby from a critical and gendered perspective that examines the sport from the power structures in which it is embedded.

References

Derby Roll Call. (2018). Derby roll call: Automatic derby name registration. Retrieved from: www.derbyrollcall.com/

Kihlstrom, J.F. (2010). Dissociative disorders. *Corsini Encyclopedia of Psychology*, 1–2.

Two Evils. (2014). Rollergirls. Retrieved from: www.twoevils.org/rollergirls/

Women's Flat Track Derby Association. (2016). Frequently asked questions. Retrieved from: https://wftda.org/faq

5   Why derby? Why now?

Roller derby as rebellion and emancipation

Earlier chapters discussed various aspects of roller derby's resurgence, from rules and league structure to three hurdles that would seemingly prevent women from playing, the extensive time and financial commitment, as well as the promise of serious injury. Other chapters examined the numerous benefits the women gain from playing, including improved physical and mental health, increased self-confidence, a larger social circle, new female friendships, as well as benefits tied to playing under a derby persona. I turn my focus in this chapter to consider what modern day roller derby means for broader issues of gender and power by attempting to answer the overarching question of my research study: *Why derby? Why now?*

Gender as social construct and moving target

As I explain in Chapter 1, this study uses the definition of gender as a social construct. Gender as socially constructed refers to gender as "an emergent feature of social situations: both as an outcome of and a rationale for various social arrangements, and as a means of legitimating one of the most fundamental divisions of society" (West & Zimmerman, 2002, p. 4). Moreover, gender is what defines our "roles, rights, and responsibilities and obligations" (Vasiljević, Marling, & Örtenblad, 2017, p. 4). In other words, gender has been "nurtured" into us by socially constructed institutions that serve to divide the sexes.

The process through which individuals learn about gender norms is known as gender socialization. Because gender is a "historical phenomenon" (Alvesson & Billing, 2009, p. 9), gender norms change across time and within and between cultures. Thus, as Wharton (2012) says, to study gender is to take "an interest in a moving target" (p. 103).

Not only is gender a moving target, but to study gender as an essential construct through which entire cultures and societies are organized is itself a political act (Alvesson & Billing, 2009). This is especially true considering that not only are people socialized to enact differing gender roles, but those roles confer different social statuses. Vasiljević et al. (2017) explain, "Gender difference is also a hierarchy in which practices and behaviors associated with men have historically been valued higher than those linked to women, resulting in women's disadvantaged status in all spheres of society" (p. 4). Thus, to "see" gender roles and norms, and the power structures inherent in the gendered socialization of men and women, is to call attention to the inequalities and inequities entrenched in a gendered society, and to search for opportunities to subvert this domination.

A critical-interpretive lens

Through a layered perspective of gender as a historical and social construct, coupled with a critical-interpretive lens, I attempted to answer my overarching question: *Why derby? Why now?* Viewing roller derby from an interpretive lens means that I seek a "deeper" understanding of the lived experiences of the women who play roller derby (Corbin & Strauss, 2008; Rubin & Rubin, 2005). This interpretive perspective is especially important as an outsider who does not play derby. Before I can critique or provide commentary on a site with which I have no personal lived experience, I must research and investigate as much as I am able. Weaving critical theory with an interpretive perspective moves beyond gaining a deeper understanding by leaving open the possibility of criticizing "ideas and meanings expressed within social groups and situations being studied" (Alvesson & Billing, 2009, p. 43). As critical theorists aim to foreground the voices and interests of marginalized groups, a critical perspective emphasizes an inability to divorce a site of study from the power structures in which it is embedded.

Specifically, a critical lens calls on researchers to consider issues of power structures and inequalities, as well as moments of alienation or awareness and ultimately avenues of emancipation. Therefore, to answer W*hy derby? Why now?*, I call for understanding roller derby as a site of gendered resistance and rebellion and ultimately as a catalyst for awareness and an agent of emancipation. I argue that derby serves an emancipatory function due to how derby provides women with an avenue to express and free themselves, both while actively engaged in competition and across other contexts and relationships in their lives.

Derby empowers women to explore alternative gender expressions by offering a space to resist gender binaries and gender polarization. Gender polarization refers to the ways "in which behaviors and attitudes that are viewed as appropriate for men are seen as inappropriate for women and vice versa" (Ryle, 2012, p. 135). Gender polarization has two key consequences: (a) "it creates two mutually exclusive scripts for being male and female" (p. 135); in other words, what is appropriate for males will only ever be appropriate for them, and vice versa; and (b) it categorizes, even punishes, any person, male or female, who deviates from these scripts, or ideals, as "unnatural, immoral, abnormal or pathological" (Ryle, 2012, p. 135). While most individuals deviate from these mutually exclusive scripts, "nevertheless, large number of people support and aspire to these ideals and are judged according to them" (Ely & Padavic, 2007, p. 1129). Alvesson and Billing (2009) note that failing to embody these gendered ideals can produce feelings of doubt and failure, "for example, not being the right kind of parent, career-person, sexually attractive and fit, not sufficiently well-dressed and exhibiting signs of success" (p. 101).

Roller derby challenges such a binary view of gender, by disputing the existence of only two genders through the welcoming of skaters who identify along a spectrum of genders, and by disregarding scripts of appropriate male and femaleness. Moreover, derby yields sites through which athletes contest gender norms and boundaries. Thus, instead of producing and reproducing existing power structures that maintain a hierarchy privileging masculinity (and men) over femininity (and women), derby disrupts these structures in both large and incremental ways, ultimately illuminating moments of awareness and emancipation in participants' lives.

The rest of this chapter identifies various ways I argue *roller derby as a site of gendered resistance and rebellion* is a useful construct with which to view this phenomenon of its resurgence. I break my analysis into four parts:

(a) **Daughters of Title IX.** In keeping with the perspective of viewing roller derby through the critical lens of power structures, I must first address how girls and women in the United States came to access athletics in such great numbers that a phenomenon like roller derby could even exist today. I argue that roller derby's resurgence is tied directly to the 1970's landmark legislation, Title IX.

(b) **Roller derby as gendered performance.** Second, I connect derby with the perspective of gender performativity as I consider how derby provides skaters with a space to explore and experiment with a wide range of gendered expressions. Specifically, this section also explores how derby contests traditional gender socialization and disrupts the gender binary.

(c) **Empowering the disempowered.** Following the discussion of how derby is a gendered performance, I address ways derby has empowered previously disempowered and disenfranchised women. I then discuss how participants view derby as "empowering." Third, in the spirit of critical theory, I examine how derby co-constructs new roles and rituals within personal and social relationships. Specifically, I note how derby led some participants to an awareness, causing them to revisit existing relationship structures. Additionally, others use derby as an emancipatory, addicting escape. I also consider the ways derby facilitates opportunities for resistance on both micro and macro levels.

(d) **Spectacle vs. sport.** This fourth section of the chapter looks to the future of derby by considering its trajectory since its resurgence and considers the tensions between remaining an alternative, at times counterculture, sport versus the pull for legitimacy as a sport played by serious athletes. Viewing roller derby as a site of gendered resistance and rebellion explains how issues of rules, uniforms, and league design escalate to existential questions for some of the skaters about how to grow the sport in a way that meets the diverse needs of its skaters while trying to maintain the antiestablishment spirit from early in the resurgence.

Daughters of Title IX

In many ways, the resurgence of roller derby can be tied to Title IX, the legislation that opened the door to athletics for girls and women around the United States. Title IX states that: "No person in the United States shall, on the basis of sex, be excluded from participation in, be denied the benefits of, or be subjected to discrimination under any education program or activity receiving Federal financial assistance" (United States Department of Justice, 2015). Though the 37-word passage makes no mention of athletics, this is the landmark legislation that forced high schools and colleges to provide athletic opportunities to women. Title IX was first passed by President Nixon more than forty-five years ago in 1972. It faced numerous legal challenges, with many seeking to exempt athletics from the law. In 1978, the deadline for high schools and colleges to comply passed. Another key date is 1979, when the United States Department of Health, Education, and Welfare presented the final interpretation of the law, which included the "three-pronged test" designed to provide further guidance on what constitutes compliance with the law. In the forty-five years since the bill first became law, the country has seen "a 545% increase in the percentage of women playing college sports and a 990% increase in the percentage of women playing high school sports" (Brooke-Marciniak & Varona, 2016). Put simply, prior to Title IX, one in 27 girls played sports. In 2016, that that number was two in five (Olmstead, 2016). As the National Coalition for Women and Girls in Education (2012) argues, "Huge gains in the number of female athletes demonstrate the key principle underlying the legislation: Women and girls have an equal interest in sports and deserve equal opportunities to participate" (p. 8).

Decades of research into Title IX's effects have indicated countless life-altering benefits for female athletes. As Kotschwar, with the World Economic Forum (2014), explained, "Girls who play sports do better in school, suffer fewer health problems, achieve more in areas dominated by men, such as science, and hold better jobs as adults" (p. 1). Moreover, "girls who play sports in school tend to do better in school, resort less to drugs, have better health, and have better workplace outcomes than those who do not" (Kotschwar, 2014, p. 2). They are also less likely to engage in risky behavior, including smoking, doing drugs, and sexual activity:

> adolescent female athletes have lower rates of both sexual activity and unintended pregnancy than their non-athlete counterparts. This is true for white, African American, and Latina athletes.
>
> (NCWGE, 2017, p 5)

Clearly, the "huge gains," not only in the number of female athletes but in the ways sports impact their lives, suggest that much of the landscape of the country has similarly been transformed by 1972's shift in public policy. Thus, merely opening the doors of athletics to girls has an emancipatory effect. While modern roller derby could have had a following without this landmark legislation, the deep well of talented, athletic women looking to play sports after high school and college would not exist without Title IX.

As a daughter of Title IX myself, one of the saddest aspects of my study is hearing some of the older interviewees gush about derby as the first sport they ever played. While they love derby and appreciate the opportunity to play, they are keenly aware of the opportunities they missed due to their age and lack of access. In contrast, my younger participants, athletes their entire lives, flocked to derby as adults precisely *because* they are aware of the value athletics contributes to their lives. Eliza explained this perspective:

> Prior to me going into derby, I was running and that was okay, but I kind of felt like something was missing from my life, and I think part of it was because I used to be very athletic and in team sports, and so I have always kind of just missed that, and I haven't done anything since college. And so I think that this was kind of the answer that I was looking for.

Unfortunately, opportunities for team sports is (perceived to be) less available to women post-college than it is for men. For example, while men might be able to round up a pickup basketball game in various gyms or parks, women might not have that sort of access to fellow athletes. Natalie spoke to this lack of sports for women post-college:

> I grew up playing all kinds of sports. I got to college-age, like 22, it's like what do you really do after that? You either go professional or recreational. You get a group of girls together and play volleyball at the rec center (laughs.) Or you go professional which is really hard to do in most sports . . . There are not many sports like that for women right now.

Therefore, Natalie is like thousands of women who searched for athletic and competitive opportunities post-college and found derby.

Overall, participants noted that derby has served as a positive force in athletics by enabling women to participate in sports in ways previously withheld from them, both because of their age or because of a dearth of post-college highly competitive team sports. In short, roller derby – in terms of size and athleticism – would not exist were it not for Title IX's groundbreaking civil rights legislation that shattered barriers for girls and women in the United States. One of the fruits of that legislation, forty-five years later, is roller derby. I shift from this discussion of Title IX to considering derby as a site of gendered performance.

Roller derby as gendered performance

For some women across the world, merely playing sports is an act of rebellion. For many girls and women in the United States, who have had access to sports thanks to Title IX, athletics themselves might not serve as an act of rebellion. However, as I discussed previously, women-as-athletes confronts, and has confronted, people's traditional gender roles. The more physical the sport, the greater the acts of masculinity the athletes embody, the greater the resistance from outsiders, including those who question women's femininity, and often their sexuality, merely because these women dare to engage in athletic contests.

West and Zimmerman (2002) define gender as "an emergent feature of social situations: both as an outcome of and a rationale for various social arrangements, and as a means of legitimating one of the most fundamental divisions of society" (p. 4). In other words, gender has been "nurtured" into us by socially constructed institutions that serve to divide the sexes. West and Zimmerman's (1987) foundational article, *Doing Gender*, focused on the ramifications of "doing gender" by noting how the ways individuals enact their gender identity are both the result and the reproduction of larger social and power structures.

In a similarly groundbreaking work, Judith Butler (1990) used the term *gender performativity* to describe the ways that men and women "perform" gender in their daily lives, both alone and while interacting with others. Butler (1990) famously argued that gender is "real only to the extent that it is performed" (p. 278). Regardless if using the term "doing" or "performing" gender, the underlying argument is that enacting gender is, in many ways, outside of the actor's control; preexisting, powerful, social structures reinforce dominant norms of what it means to be feminine and masculine, and constrain behaviors that might blur "conventional" gender boundaries by teaching us the consequences of unconventional gender performativity. Thus, gendered enactments carry with them elements of both agency and complicity (Grindstaff & West, 2010).

I argue that it is these dominating power structures that lead some women to derby because the sport provides gender transgression zones, or figurative spaces to explore gender expression. Gender transgression zones challenge "gender-typed behaviors, or between what's seen as appropriate for boys and appropriate for girls" (Ryle, 2012, p. 148). Although many sports may provide sites for potential transgressions for women, the nature of derby disrupts gender norms by specifically calling for women to challenge propriety through physical contact and collisions.

While gender-as-performative refers to the ways everyone performs gender in our daily lives, from our gait and vocal features to how we dress, the chores we do (or refuse to do) and the careers we enter – or avoid, scholars have looked to drag as a complex site of study for the ways – like derby – it foregrounds notions of gender performativity into our consciousness (See Levitt, et al., 2018; Berbary & Johnson, 2016). For example, in their famous ethnography of a drag cabaret, Rupp and Taylor (2003) argued that drag serves as a form of protest because of three key criteria of social movements: (a) collective identities, (b) contestations, and (c) intentionality. Roller derby easily satisfies the criterion of a collective identity, or a sense of "we-ness" at both the in-group and out-group levels. Rupp and Taylor (2003) argue that collective identities are formed "among members of marginalized groups in networks and free spaces outside the surveillance of dominant groups" (p. 219). Throughout this book, I have called attention to the ways that derby has built community and international networks. Of course, skaters invite members of dominant groups to their public bouts, but at that point, I argue their collective identity – as well as their individual derby identities – provides a sense of cover.

Second, like drag, I argue that derby is a contested performance where symbols, identities, and behaviors "conveyed by a cultural performance subvert rather than maintain dominant relations of power" (Rupp & Taylor, 2003, p. 217). Relatedly, and regarding intentionality, Rupp and Taylor (2003) write: "To what extent are drag queens intentionally thinking and acting consciously about goals and strategies for challenging dominant constructions of masculinity, femininity and the gendered heterosexual family?" (p. 218). Throughout this book, I have noted how the desire to play a sport does not explain the enthusiasm, or the evangelism, with which the women gushed about derby. Instead, they spoke of ways derby helps them rebel against societal norms of femininity and masculinity, by providing gender transgression zones. Thus, if Butler describes gender as performance (and the early days of Roller derby's resurgence, especially with its costumes, alter egos, and theatrics, was itself certainly a performance), and Rupp and Taylor (2003) argue that these gendered performances can be politicalized, then we must look at roller derby as a gendered political performance, i.e., ways that gender and roller derby function to subvert traditional gender scripts (see Rupp, Taylor, & Shapiro, 2010). The rest of this section examines ways derby as a performance challenges and reifies gender roles in a way that makes sense for participants.

"We're not taught as young girls": contesting "traditional" gender socialization

A number of women mentioned that, even with access to athletics as young girls, girls in general are not socialized to enact traditionally masculine characteristics of aggression, ambition, or competition to the extent of playing a contact sport like roller derby. Rae sees this socialization in action with newcomers who slowly relearn what they're capable of:

> I've seen so many women try out for derby and [they say] "I don't know. I don't know if I can do that. I don't think I could get out there and be hit or hit somebody." They try out, they train really hard, and then they have their first bout. Something changes in them on the track. They can do it. And I think as women we're not really taught as young girls that we can do something of this nature.

Helena agreed: "At least for me, and I saw this with a lot of women, a lot of women don't necessarily have the self-confidence or maybe they're too afraid to show their power and to show that they're strong, while with roller derby, you can be whatever you wanted to be." Emma sees gender socialization as teaching women to doubt themselves, a trait that derby helps women overcome:

> As women we always doubt ourselves, so I think that the role of the team is to build each other up as much as possible so that people can achieve the potential that maybe they never knew what they had, or doubted that they could achieve.

In other words, derby encourages – whether deliberately or as a natural consequence of participation – females to unlearn the scripts they had memorized regarding how to perform femininity. Bridgett wants young female fans who come to bouts to discover more complex modes of femininity, to see that they, too, can be both feminine and yet aggressive and competitive:

> [Girls] can be really pretty and sweet but they can just totally just kick ass and I think that is such an empowering message to women. I mean, not that you have to be pretty and nice if you don't want to be, but it's kind of like that you CAN be a bad ass – aggressive, assertive woman and that's great.

Indeed, Lucy sees gender socialization as one reason why so many women see the need for alter egos or derby personas. She views these personas as giving women permission to be different and aggressive, to rebel against how they are socialized:

> It's less having an alter ego and a different identity and a reason to be different and aggressive. We're not socialized to be that way as women . . . [Derby] gives you permission to embrace these different aspects that we're not necessarily what we're socialized to express publicly.

In other words, women need this permission – as well as a gender transgression zone – to explore aspects of their personalities they are not encouraged to express publicly. Lucy concluded by acknowledging how women are discouraged from veering off script in their "regular" lives: "We all have our different roles and our different scripts that we follow." Likewise, Eliza thinks derby is fun, but it also allows skaters to explore different sides to themselves: "Roller derby is, first and foremost, just a lot of fun. It is a lot of fun, and you get to be aggressive, you get to be all of the things that you might not necessarily get to be."

Disrupting the gender binary

Joanna illustrated how roller derby makes skaters appear more masculine: "You seem more masculine when you do play a heavier sport like this. Whether it's hockey or competitive soccer . . . We're talking about full-blown, hardcore [sport]."

In an interesting contrast, Kate, who joined roller derby at 40, learned how to be *feminine* because of the sport, though she has played other contact sports:

> I learned how to become feminine at forty. Roller derby taught me how to be feminine for the first time in my life. I had played soccer and ultimate my whole life and I've always been the fumbling awkward jock that didn't think you could be a jock and also be feminine. My brain didn't go there.

Kate explained that she felt this way because she joined roller derby back when a player could explore her sexuality more with her derby persona as well as how she dressed for the bout (e.g., fishnet stockings, short shorts, etc.). She continued:

> So I appreciated that it was as sassy as it was when I joined . . . It's funny, I had done the reverse. When I started playing I . . . [wore] no sass. My teammates were sass all over the place. Then, the work that I did on myself was "Hey, stop being such a jock, stop taking it so seriously. Have fun. Get some booty shorts."

Kate added that she eventually went back to her original black stretch pants, but held out longer than her initially "sassier" teammates did.

Both Joanna's and Kate's quotations regarding derby as masculine *or* feminine speak to the complex nature of gender. Gender is not some binary construct that one can map onto a person: X is a masculine behavior, Y is a feminine behavior. Rather the performance of gender is the result of being rewarded or reprimanded for acting in ways that support another's concept of what it means to be a man, or a woman. As such, derby allows skaters to rebel and rewrite their own gendered scripts. The next section presents one of the most common ways derby encourages women to rethink these scripts.

"There's no 'sorry' in derby"

The most common "deprogramming" women discussed was teaching each other not to apologize when making contact. Eliza said one aspect of the contact in derby was learning not to say sorry: "Yeah, that actually took me a while, in derby, I was always like, 'Sorry, sorry,' and they were like, 'Stop saying that! You don't need to apologize!' And it's taken me a while." Julie has the same experience: "At least in our league, we say, 'There's no 'sorry' in derby,' because you're gonna go in to hit someone and trip them once in a while, and they'll fall, and so what, that's part of the game (laughs)." Joanna notes that she and other skaters apologize all the time: "It happens all the time. It's always like, there is no sorry in derby. There is no sorry in derby. People still [say it], no matter what. You know I used to do it myself."

As a former athlete, I remember being taught by coaches – and then telling various teammates (and a few opponents) not to apologize. Apologizing is ubiquitous in women's sports as females are socialized to be kind and to cooperate, not to compete physically. Unless this behavior is unlearned, with a sport like derby, a skater would be apologizing incessantly. On the other hand, by teaching females that this behavior is inappropriate within an athletic context, the lesson that femininity is problematic, or substandard, is reinforced. These lessons further the idea that sports are masculine, and for men, unless women "do" sports in a set, prescriptive manner.

This section examined ways derby operates as a gendered performance that contests one's gender socialization by encouraging participants to explore different behaviors and scripts for enacting one's gender. The next section discusses various ways participants found derby to be empowering.

Empowering the disempowered

Just as Title IX empowered millions of females by providing access to athletics, roller derby empowers women, both in general, as the women often used the word "empowering" to describe the sport, and by creating moments of awareness (via revisiting some relationships) and emancipation (via providing an addicting escape as well as a successful women-centric organization).

Roller derby as empowering

Participants commonly referred to roller derby as "empowering." Sarah called it "hugely empowering." Derby gave her the confidence to "stand up for [herself] more" and quit corporate America:

> I needed to quit my jobs desperately because I was too far into corporate America and miserable and [derby] really empowered me to say,

"I can do this. I can do anything" and go out on my own. I've been much happier and frankly, making more money.

Basma sees the entire sport as empowering women in a way that spills over into their non-derby lives. She said that her biggest takeaway of her time with derby:

> has just been the empowerment of the whole sport itself, just seeing the transformation that somebody takes once they initially start and the confidence that just day by day, each time that you put on those skates. As you go out there the confidence just grows . . . It's a confidence that you carry with yourself even when you aren't skating in your everyday life.

After Bridgett described how signing autographs for young girls was a surreal experience, I asked her what she hopes those young fans learn from watching her play. She responded with a list of hopes: "That roller derby is empowering and boosts confidence . . . And I hope they take away knowing there's all these awesome women out there that give back to the community and do all this for fun." She also hopes they become inspired to keep derby alive: "And I kind of hope that they go away wanting to actually play derby so we can keep this going for generations." Natalie finds the sport empowering because of how far she has come as a skater. At the time I interviewed her, she played on the highest ranked team in the world, though she started on a lower ranking team within her league before advancing to the travel team.

> As a woman, it's been empowering because it's the fastest growing sport, but personally it's been empowering because I grew with the sport as an athlete, because now I'm on the number one team in the world, but I started on a low ranking [home] team.

Roller derby empowers skaters in general by increasing one's confidence. This increased confidence leads some women to an awareness or an awakening about certain romantic or familial relationships.

Revisiting relationships

I asked all the women how people in their lives reacted to their participation in derby. All of the skaters with children said their children are proud of their mothers. A number of women shared that their families have been supportive, including their spouses, parents, and grandparents. For example,

Eliza's husband is proud of her: "My husband is very supportive of it. He is very encouraging, and he's very proud of me being in derby." Rae said her husband loves it so much he usually buys tickets and brings his friends or clients to bouts:

> He loves it. He absolutely loves it. The last bout that we had, he bought two of our big boxes [of seats] and brought a bunch of fellow service industry people in to watch the bout and then some business clients in to watch the bout too. He loves it. He thinks it's great.

Maude's mom and dad "tune into" her games and travel to see her compete, even sponsoring her trading card:

> My mom always tunes in, watches all my games, every time they're streamed. Both my parents were at regionals last year. And then they both flew down to nationals . . . They love it. They're my sponsors. We get trading cards, and my parents and my sister and my brother-and-law, they all sponsored me for my trading card.

Dana's boyfriend travels to away games with her and often finds himself blending into the community:

> He travels with me to away games and it's just a really nice community that he can then find himself in as well, whether it's tear down the track, which he hates, or sitting in the stands and drinking, which he really likes. He's supportive of it; whereas a lot of people are not.

Dana described previous, less supportive boyfriends. Ultimately, she chose derby:

> I had boy friends who refused to come to games because they didn't want to see me hurt and didn't like it when I would go and try to be intimate and have bruises on me. They would be like "You need to stop" and I'm like "no" and so it was either roller derby or this dude, and I was like "I'm picking roller derby." Which is kind of awesome. But there are a lot of girls like that that have lost relationships over the sport.

While he does not like to see his wife injured, Lynn's husband is so supportive, he lends his photography and graphic design skills to her league:

> He thinks it's awesome (laughs). He was so worried that I was going to get hurt. I did get hurt a couple of times because I'm pretty klutzy.

And I had to keep convincing him, "No, wait, I skate better than I walk, I promise." But he thinks it's fantastic.

Sophia's husband gave a fist bump in the air when he overheard her mention him during our phone interview. She said:

> He's been really, really supportive. I'm very fortunate. He's standing here pumping his fist in the air (laughs). No, seriously, I'm fortunate . . . I said I wanted to do it, and he said, "Oh, that sounds like a good idea."

She contrasts that to teammates who did not have such supportive partners. She does not lay blame for their divorces on derby, but suggests derby was a catalyst:

> There's a few girls that don't get that type of support from husbands . . . [Husbands] just don't get [derby]. I even know two girls that actually got divorces. Not to say derby caused it, but it was maybe the catalyst.

Natalie described the term "derby widow" as the partner who gets left behind because a woman is always doing something derby-related. During her time playing derby, she has seen the sport as separating couples:

> Over the years I've seen a lot of relationships come and go and a lot of relationships fail because of derby. I guess that could happen in any kind of extra-curricular activity you're doing, but derby just seems to . . . kind of separate people, which is weird.

Natalie thinks it's because seeing their wives or partners doing something fulfilling can breed resentment:

> I feel like so many women want to fulfill that athletic side in their life, and they're fulfilling it, so they're really, I wouldn't say living the dream, but they're happy and they're doing something that makes them happy. And if your spouse is sitting at home and they're not following their dream or they're not doing anything, they kind of build up resentment, like "Oh she's doing what she loves, and I wish I could do what I love."

She uses the example of her ex-husband: "With my ex, he was a musician, he was pursuing the music industry for as long as I've known him, since he was 14, and he wasn't going anywhere, and here I am progressing and progressing." She does not blame derby for her divorce but says they "really, really grew apart." When I asked Mary Ellen about any negatives from derby, she directly mentions the separation from her husband:

> I'm separated now, in the beginning [derby] was actually a challenge to our relationship . . . It is a big change, I think, for a spouse to watch their wife go through all these changes all of a sudden. It's a very different lifestyle, the derby lifestyle, and of course being away so much.

Husbands and partners are not the only ones who struggle to understand derby. A few parents have been less than enthusiastic. While Rae has other family members who are as supportive as her husband, Rae's father does not attend bouts anymore:

> Then my dad is not a big fan of roller derby for the most part because of his religious background. He doesn't feel like it's very family friendly. That's been hard . . . he doesn't like the [derby] names. He doesn't find that to be very appealing. My dad used to come watch me play roller derby, but he stopped watching me play. That hurts a little bit, but it doesn't stop me because it's something I'm passionate about.

Another skater mentioned that her parents came to a bout and did not know what to say, so they just left and did not talk to their daughter. Alexis said: "My parents, (pause) they came to one bout and I don't know, I don't think they were very into it, they left immediately after and didn't even talk to me (laughs). So that was kind of weird." Though her brother is supportive, it is unfortunate that her parents were not as enthusiastic, as Alexis does not have a lot of people she would invite to her bouts: "I'm not super social, I'm pretty scared of people, so I don't invite a lot of people to my stuff (laughs). And I don't have a lot of (pause) friends I would consider inviting to that kind of stuff." Natalie, who moved to a large East Coast city specifically for derby, had trouble explaining the move to her parents. As she explained:

> [My parents] said quote "It's a hobby, why would you move for a hobby?" I was like "It's more than a hobby, you don't understand, someday it's going to be really big and we're going to get paid for it and all kinds of stuff, and what else am I going to try to be the best at?"

Especially in American culture, the idea of quitting your job to move cross country to try out for a top derby team in pretty unthinkable. Natalie likes to think she blazed a trail of sorts:

> I don't know if [started is] the right word, but I think I kind of made it okay for other girls to be like "Yea, I can move just to [large city] just to play roller derby," even though it's not my paying job.

Kimberly's parents were likewise concerned when they drove three hours with her to a major city to buy skates: "My parents watched me drop $600 for this sport I had never tried, on roller skates which I had never been on. They were VERY concerned that I was wasting time." She told me that as they watched her develop, and learned more about derby, they became her biggest fans: "But as they watched me get more fit, as they've seen it become more popular, now that they've been to bouts, and they've seen that it's actually a sport and that we are competitive, they are fully behind it." In fact, her older brother now coaches her team and her parents wear shirts to bouts saying "[Derby name's] Dad" and "[Derby name's] Mom."

This section illustrated how various family members react to seeing women they love play a sport they love, and a sport that for many, changed their lives. Those with supportive, enthusiastic partners know how "fortunate" they are as they know plenty of their teammates have ended serious relationships while in derby. For some, their newfound confidence pushes them to question the status quo of certain relationships. In this way, derby provides what critical theorists call an "awareness" in one's life. Critical theorists also consider the ways one finds emancipation from dominating power structures. The next two sections focus on two emancipative features of derby: (a) derby as an addictive escape and (b) derby as providing a woman-centric organization.

The emancipatory function of derby

Because so many participants referred to derby as "addicting" and as an "escape," I came to see roller derby as a site of emancipation for women, both in the ways derby "frees" the women while they play, and in the way derby's benefits spill over into the rest of their lives. For example, Julie expressed: "Once I started doing [derby], I think I just became sort of addicted to it. I really cannot picture derby not being a part of my life." Maura describes derby as a "wonderful way" to "express yourself" and "put your feelings on the track," adding:

For a short bit, you can have these brief battles and come off as a winner or loser, and learn from that and just come and play a game . . . It's its own world. It's a great place to escape sometimes.

When I asked Mary Ellen why she plays, she said: "I will sum it up for you in one sentence . . . It's just that escape from everyday life. It really is – it's an outlet." Maya views derby as an addicting outlet because of the challenges: "I cut out every other expense I possibly could in my life . . . there's just something ADDICTIVE about it, I mean you look forward to it all week, you get EXCITED to be met with challenges."

Of derby, Eliza described derby as "me time" and as: "a little addictive, I think. You can't go into derby halfway. You can't dip a toe in there . . . It's a great release, especially [for those] who work a lot, that they have something." When Eliza plays, she clears her mind of everything at work and home. She knows she is not the only American who needs an outlet like she has: "Americans are one of the hardest-working work forces in the world, and I think that it can take its toll. People need time for themselves, especially if you're just slaving away at the office." Eliza, like many women believes that everyone needs something just for themselves. Tina agreed:

[Derby is a] total escape from reality. It's like throw caution to the wind and get the skates on and just get out there and go up against the big girls and just do your thing. Be professional during the day, be a mommy, be a wife but you know what, I have my own thing too. I'm this roller derby chick and it's FUN it's cool. It makes me feel like I'm doing something for MYSELF and in turn, that's only gonna benefit my family and my kids and my husband.

Shannon used the term sanctuary to describe what derby has given her:

No matter what's going on in their real life, derby's like this sanctuary. You can always go to practice, you can have a really nice hard, fun workout with people who really genuinely care about you, and come out of it feeling a little bit better. Your life problem is still there, but you feel a little bit more ready to deal with them.

Similarly, Emma sees derby as giving her a place to work through bad days. She says if she has a bad day, derby can "de-stress your life" and helps one "get away from it all." She added that if she has a bad day:

the first thing I want to do – I want to go to practice . . . So I wanna keep that in my life, because what would I have done otherwise (laughs)? I would have gone and cried in my pillow by myself alone. And then I wouldn't have felt any better.

Emma summarized why this outlet is so important: "So yeah. I think that's what keeps us (laughs), keeps me going." Bridgett compares roller derby to the movie *Fight Club* in the sense that people lack "personal connections" and thus need "outlets for their frustration and aggression":

> [Derby] just kind of reminds me about the movie *Fight Club*. I think that the world we live in is so stressful and so intense and often times so lacking in personal connections, especially in the white collar corporate setting I think that people need outlets for their frustration and aggression and they need something to make them feel this sense of joy and accomplishment and confidence and power.

Bridgett thinks that the harder it is to find these outlets means one needs it even more: "I think in the world we live in, it's like even though it makes it really difficult to have all of these things, we need them more."

While alter egos and derby personas provide one kind of escape, these excerpts illustrate how derby provides another type of emancipating escape because the sport provides a release and a sanctuary from the daily grind, however brief, for many of the skaters. The next section analyzes how derby serves a second emancipatory purpose by being a woman-centric organization, which contrasts the rest of their lives.

This is ours: we built it: derby as empowering, women-centric organization

Many of the participants noted the importance of being part of a woman-centric organization, both because of how their leagues are run, and because the resurgence centered around women's derby first with men's derby existing as an outgrowth of the women's sport. As such, there are unique characteristics of women's derby. Lucy illustrated these differences: "[Derby] grew into this thing that was uniquely female dominated and that didn't have an exclusively male mold to emulate. There are very few sports that can say that, particularly team sports." As a result, roller derby has

> this culture of dominance by women – a culture that grew out of women and women's network and empowering to women . . . It also allows

them to fully be physical and aggressive in a completely appropriate way that was not emulating men.

She points out that men's derby actually emulates the mold women skaters created:

> The men's roller derby movement is men emulating the mold that women formed in this particular sport in its unique way. When men's derby first started . . . there were a lot of women in roller derby who were very much against men playing roller derby. It's kind of this proprietary feeling, that ownership and a need to protect it. "This is ours. Men have all the sports. Why should we let you guys come in and now you're just going to make it manly, just like everything else and take it away from us?"

Yet, Lucy argued that this perspective flies in the face of derby's values of inclusivity. She points out that the men who play men's roller derby found the sport through coaching and volunteering for the women's leagues and aspired to be like the women:

> It's not like random men came through women's roller derby and said, "We're going to do that now," and started their own thing . . . They weren't just swooping in and taking it away. They were learning and growing and aspiring to be like these women athletes.

Indeed, a few participants mentioned how they now coach or referee in the men's leagues, after being approached by the players. Lucy refers to women as architects of the derby landscape as a reversal of sporting norms. She concluded: "I can't think of any other sport that has that inversion either – between the histories in the genders." I spoke with Audra the night after a bout. She described playing in front of huge crowds as "amazing" and added: "One of the things that I love about roller derby, is it's the only sport I know of that's really a woman's world and the men either ref or cheer and that's pretty much it. So that's really nice." Julie also feels pride in building the resurgence of roller derby as women-first such that it's "roller derby" and then "men's roller derby" unlike other sports where people say "basketball" and "women's basketball":

> It's just really cool that this is one thing that women have that does not have the label of men on it, like women's golf, women's basketball, women's this. There's always that modifier, but roller derby is ours. It's not "women's roller derby." It's something that we've owned from the

beginning, we've made it huge. Now when you see men's teams, they have the modifier, you know: "men's" roller derby. It's the only sport I know of that's like that. And it's really cool that we built that.

While Lucy and some welcome the inclusivity of men's derby, Emma was one of the participants who was skeptical that men's derby would not ultimately harm women's derby:

> I just kind of feel like, you know, that roller derby is a sport for women by women, and that if men start playing it, then it's going to start to be about men. They have every other sport in the world geared towards them, was made for them, made by them. This is the one sport women have where it's about women playing . . . I just feel like it's going to be bad for women's roller derby to have men's roller derby, because what if people aren't interested in women's roller derby anymore? Or if the public gets turned on to men's roller derby? We struggled so hard to get our own fans, and what if people are like, "Wow, women's roller derby is, like, ridiculous, but men's roller derby is so much better!"

Kimberly finds that this pride in ownership entails a large responsibility. Unlike other sports she has played, she finds a number of skaters are concerned about being known as the team that plays strategy, which means exploiting loopholes. She articulated:

> It seems to me that in derby there's a lot of women who don't want to be the team that plays STRATEGY. They want to match athletics. So it's been an interesting discussion with our team about, "Can we do that? Is that OK? Are we going to offend somebody?"

Kimberly sees this concern as being unique to derby, and not for example, rugby: "And that's something that I think is really unique to derby. I don't think that as a rugby player I was ever concerned about whether the other team would think of what we did was honorable or not (laughs)." She thinks this trait stems from the grassroots nature of derby, specifically that women did not begin playing a long-standing men's sport with predetermined rules. Thus, she senses that derby is growing with what she refers to as a "moral compass" along with the competitive nature of a sport:

> I think part of that is because it is a sport that's developing and I think the other part is because it's a sport that's developing that's mostly women. (pause) I think women sort of tend to play roles in society where we're you know, parents and mothers, and we're teaching other

people about MORALS and VALUES. And I think that that translates heavily into this new sport . . . We're at the sort of, the bottom the grass-roots part of the sport and were thinking you know, "How do we want the sport to look in 10 years? How do we want it to look in 20 years?" the decisions we make now affect that later.

Sarah looks at all the good derby does in their communities and sees its charitable actions as evidence that women built the sport:

> You know, you can tell that this is a women's homegrown sport because only a bunch of a women would dedicate 20 hours a week of their lives, all this time and energy, and say, "Oh and we have to do good in the process." It's not just about us, it's about the community too, and I love that . . . No one else is doing that.

Sarah also views derby's success as evidence women should be running the world: "This just tells me that women really should run the world, that we do good things when we are empowered." Rae likewise sees derby as changing the world:

> It's not even just changing our country. It's changing the world. It's amazing. It's funny that you mentioned [others] being evangelical about derby because I am – It's our worship. The House of Derby, that's where we go to get rid of our woes and for pick-me-ups and to celebrate.

This section outlined the pride women have in being part of a grassroots sport that is also part social movement. Though all organizations have their faults and weaknesses, derby, in its current form, seems to have found a way for stereotypical masculine and feminine values to coexist despite being embedded in a larger patriarchal, hyper individualized, neoliberal system, a system which undermines genuine efforts to consider ways that gender and racial equality and equity have forestalled or even backslid (see Arendt & Buzzanell, 2017). It is in this utopic-like sporting community that participants find moments of emancipation in the joy they find from derby as well as moments of awareness when they realize they have missed out on benefits of athletic participation or female friendships due to their age and/or being socialized to compete with each other.

Thus, I argue that derby aligns nicely with Mumby, Thomas, Martí, and Seidl's (2017) four I's of resistance, specifically insurrection, which Mumby et al. (2017) define as a macro form of public resistance, by daring to challenge ideas of sport, gender, and organizing. Derby as a sport and as a body of empowered women collectively rebels against patriarchal structures My data suggest that this collective rebellion spills over into individual acts of questioning and resistance in many of the skaters' lives, what Mumby et al. (2017) refer to as insubordination, or public forms of micro-resistance.

Following this discussion of how derby empowers, emancipates, and facilitates resistance, I now turn to the future of derby by examining the tension between maintaining the alternative, counterculture elements of the sport with a push from inside the community to mainstream the sport to gain legitimacy from outsiders.

"Spectacle vs. sport"

After illustrating the ways derby is not only a gendered performance, but also a site of gendered resistance and rebellion, I now discuss the future of derby by considering its trajectory since the resurgence. Participants discussed the tension in trying to maintain the grassroots, kitsch, and counterculture elements of the sport while striving for legitimacy as serious athletes engaged in competitive athletic endeavors. Viewing roller derby as a site of gendered resistance and rebellion explains how issues of rules, league design, derby names, and other theatrics escalate to existential questions for some of the skaters about how to grow the sport in a way that meets the diverse needs of its skaters while trying to maintain the subversive spirit.

Tutus, fishnets, drag queens, and stroller derby

When discussing the progression of the sport, participants tended to fall into three camps: pushing to mainstream the sport, ambivalence about its trajectory, and lamenting the new changes. Regardless of how the women felt, a tension exists from the need to grow the sport in a way that keeps the game exciting enough to build a loyal fan base that every league needs as revenue.

Julie followed derby in her area from its arrival, even though she waited a few years to try out herself. She described the progression of the sport as "punk rock and DIY [do it yourself]" with DJs spinning underground music and skaters playing in mismatched uniforms and even corsets to women playing in "actual clothes that make sense to roller skate in." But now, derby is

> all moving towards kind of feeling a little bit more legitimate as a sport, but then it affects everything, because you have the uniforms that actually look like uniforms, versus "everybody vaguely try and get a blue shirt that matches and ya know puffy paint your name on the back."

Not only are teams buying uniforms at "real uniform stores," but today's skater needs to be in terrific shape if she hope to compete:

> People are cross training which is something, ya know, six years ago if you said, "Oh yeah I'm gonna cross train," people's idea of cross training was like probably don't get drunk the night before the bout, like that's probably cross training.

Some of the women I interviewed had been playing long enough that they not only experienced the shift toward standardized uniforms, but they also played under more than one rule set. Some saw the evolution of the rules as a positive change in order to address, or close, loopholes that some teams exploited. Others welcomed a unified rule set initially because it made playing teams across the United States, and eventually internationally, possible. On the other hand, one rule set threatened fan bases because seasoned teams learned how to exploit the rules in a way that helped them win bouts at the expense of keeping fans entertained. Specifically, the rule set in use around 2011 gave rise to "stroller derby", or a *much* slower pace of play that forward-thinking teams developed as a strategy. While it was advantageous for a team to play "stroller derby", it drove fans away because skaters essentially blocked each other while standing still. While a usual jam might include numerous laps around the track, teams playing stroller derby might only move a few feet. Ruth explained the effect of stroller derby on fans: "There'd been a lot of pushback from the fans who come for big hits and 30-point jams. THAT'S what's fun to watch. Not people standing still looking at each other." While skaters are not paid and they pay to play, leagues still rely on fan revenue from their bouts and thus must find a balance between athleticism and entertainment as the sport grows. Unfortunately, leagues lost untold legions of fans while they waited for the arrival of the next rule set that ended stroller derby.

Shannon is one participant who felt ambivalent, or conflicted, about the changes to the sport. When I interviewed her, she described playing under older rules and reminisced over the days when a drag queen helped the league by running the penalty box:

> When I got in there, we had a drag queen running our penalty box. It was all just a big show, you know? Everything was still very real, we were still very much out there playing a full-contact sport getting injured, but it was – I mean, the rules were so different, and that's something I find interesting about the evolution of the sport . . . Whether it's for the better or now, it depends on the person you're talking to, but it's been

very cool to have been in a sport for so long to have seen the evolution, because I don't think people who have just joined completely understand. And they get upset with a rule or something, but they haven't seen all the struggles that we've gone through in all these years to get the rules to where they are now.

Thus, while Shannon can appreciate the evolution of the rules, she feels ambivalent on the push to mainstream. For example, on the question of whether she would like to see roller derby become an Olympic sport someday, she replied: "(laughs) That's such a controversial issue, I am sort of the middle ground. I see both sides and I really don't give a shit (laughs). If it progresses into an Olympic sport, that's super awesome." On the other hand, she knows that skaters would lose the agency they secured through years of building up their organization, the Women's Flat Track Derby Association, as another agency, USA Roller Sports, competes under different rules and is the organization recognized by the United States Olympic Committee. She explained:

> You know, we've all been working – all these leagues that I've been playing for have been working really hard to build up the WFTDA, making what it is today, rewriting these rules, getting them just right, and then USARS comes in and sort of takes these rules and is like, "Nope, we're going to play it how we feel like it, and the derby players are not going to have any say." And, you know, that kind of sucks. So I get both sides, and I just don't give a shit (laughs). I don't want to spend any time worrying about it. (laughs)

Helena is someone longing for the older days of derby. Even before she became involved officially, she remembered bouts with mascots and skaters with tutus and whips: "It just kind of makes me sad, because I feel like the mascots always seem to keep the crowd engaged." Like others, Helena criticized the impact various rule changes have had on the sport. Surprisingly, she also decried the success her league has had because it necessitated a move to a larger venue. The larger venue makes bouts less interactive with fans, which she misses. Julie, meanwhile, played with a newer team in a smaller venue where fans are mere inches from the track: "So your fans are standing on the side of the track, they're giving you high-fives as you skate by, they start to feel really connected to you." For Helena, the success of her more-established league came at a price – close interaction with fans.

The drive for legitimacy: fighting for the "soul" of derby?

Many of the skaters specifically used the word *legitimate* or *legitimacy* as they described their relationship with the sport. Brooke wants to push derby toward the mainstream out of her desire to be taken seriously. She said she hears from people who think derby is full of fake, scripted fighting, to which she said she responds: "This is real. You know, I'm not just running around, prancing around (laughs)." Bridgett has a spiel she tells people misinformed about the realness of present-day derby: "I'm like, 'We are not like that [fake fighting] anymore. We are a legitimate sport.' And then they often ask, 'Well, how is it played now?' And then I just go into my little spiel about how derby's played (sighs)."

Maura similarly wants the sport to be taken more seriously but knows it means losing some of the "soul" of derby:

> The mindset of our league is that we really want this to be a legitimate sport. We want people to see this not as a sort of novelty thing, just to be odd and different and edgy; we want this to be recognized for this athletic sport that it really is.

And yet, Maura also worries about the effects of having too many corporate sponsors and losing the "do-it-yourself" nature of the league. She described this progression as: "Kind of like it would lose some of its soul." In this desire for legitimacy coupled with a worry about unintended consequences, Maura illustrates the tension felt by many participants.

In contrast, others did not feel the tension; they only wanted legitimacy. For example, Lucy bemoaned, not the shift toward legitimacy as a sport, but that the shift is not happening quickly enough. She noted that any news coverage is relegated to culture and human interest pieces, and not the sports pages:

> We're not covered in the sports pages, we're covered in the human interest features and it's "art teacher by day, cruiser by night." It's an important part of the history of the culture. I don't run away from it, but it's just one very interesting, not necessarily shallow but one, dimension. There's a lot of other depth to [the sport] in other ways. That's what makes it I think discouraging to get just that kind of coverage.

Lucy admits that there are other sports that are not covered anywhere in the newspaper at all, but she wishes that any coverage would focus on derby as a sport – even if only in the community sports section.

In many ways, individual skaters do not have the power to stop the tide of legitimacy, for example, with regard to rules or uniforms. They have felt pressured to adopt more of a standard uniform with their teammates, i.e., abandon the tutus and fishnet stockings, sooner than they may have chosen on their own. One participant recalled targeting a skater on another team because she still wore a tutu.

Another way leagues push for legitimacy is by skating under their own names. Though I did not interview any skater from a league that exclusively skates under their own names, everyone knew such leagues exist and a few shared their opinions. Madeline saw their choice as criticizing her own, and she seemed to almost take offense at the suggestion that derby personas hurt derby: "Their reasoning [to skate under their own names] is because it makes them seem more legit. That was almost a direct quote from something I read. 'Okay, whatever. That's all you then.'" Maude thinks derby already is a legitimate sport: "I think it's a legitimate sport. I think it's completely a legitimate sport. I don't know what kind of recognition people are waiting for."

Audra does understand how some leagues view derby names as anathema to being taken seriously because the names are tied to its theatrical history:

> I mean I can understand why certain leagues are moving away from [derby names] and I think a lot of that is because it used to have this history of not being taken seriously. In the past derby was something silly that people watched on television and women want the sport to be taken seriously. But my hope is that the sport can be taken seriously but you don't have to lose all of the theatricality and sort of spectacle that is involved. To be frank, too, I think having that element helps us to sell tickets to bouts and stuff because it's the sort of larger than life, the ridiculous outfits and the names and personas and I think it sort of really gets people invested in the game.

Eliza also wants to maintain the colorful aspects of derby: "I am not a fan of trying to sterilize the sport. You know, make everything monochromatic, make everything happy and nice . . . I like the idea that we can have crazy derby names, but I don't know. Time will tell."

Brooke likewise mentioned the perception that derby names hurt the cause for legitimacy, a cause she believes in. However, Brooke also sees the sport as exciting enough for spectators to withstand the loss of the names and theatrics:

> I know that there's a push for some people kind of trying to get rid of the derby name, and I'm okay with that . . . that's cool because it is a good spectator sport, but it's a good spectator sport as a sport, not just for watching girls in, you know, tight pants and tutus and, you know, just to look at them . . . We work really hard to play, so I want . . . I think it's more important to focus on that aspect of it, the sport part, than just all of the theatrics.

Roller derby's move toward legitimacy includes not just the rules, uniforms, and athleticism of its skaters, but even the structure of various leagues. Both Eliza and Jordan described their two leagues as being analogous to a corporation. Jordan described the evolution of her league into this corporate-type structure as a result of needing to create policies as issues arose.

> There's that aspect of it right, like the sport versus spectacle sort of aspect, but there's also like (pause) the way that our league has evolved in that it has become a lot more professionally run . . . Over the years, if you're setting up as a corporation and we were deciding what our policies were and our rules were . . . if there's no policy for something then people can just do whatever they want and it takes setting certain rules, you know it takes a lot of those incidents coming up to be like, "Oh we need a policy for that." (laughs)

I asked Jordan for examples of policies they had to create, and she mentioned rules surrounding how, or whether, someone could switch home teams within their leagues or how to handle leaves of absence due to pregnancy or injury.

Women did not speak of pushing to grow the sport only for legitimacy's sake or to be taken seriously as an athlete. Many of the women were actively working to grow the sport by developing tutorials, teaching and coaching in the junior leagues, and by traveling to other leagues, both across the United States and internationally, to teach skills and strategy, and even to mentor skaters trying to establish new leagues. These unpaid and tireless efforts speak to their altruistic drive to grow the sport, even as skaters know their own time skating is limited. While many skaters would retire, or "hang up their skates," before seeing a direct impact from traveling cross country to set up leagues or conducting coaching and skaters' clinics, the rapid growth of the sport can be attributed to these efforts; in other words, redefining competition as one that gains from cooperation instead of viewing competition and sport as a zero-sum game.

However, questions of legitimacy versus maintaining the subversive, counterculture aspect of the sport reach further than merely changing the rules or wearing standardized uniforms. For the women who view roller derby as an escape and as something that imbued them with confidence and an empowerment that spilled over into their non-derby lives, mainstreaming the sport can be perceived as threatening the woman-centric communal organization that exists as evidence of alternative yet successful ways of organizing.

Thus, examining the trajectory and iterations of the sport as it develops raises significant existential questions, including asking what it means that so many women are pushing for the sport to be taken seriously, and by whose metric would they measure legitimacy. Other key questions include asking what the sport gains from efforts to legitimize. Perhaps more importantly, what does roller derby as both a sport and culture stand to lose? Moreover, on a frightening note, what would it mean for the sport and its athletes if the push to mainstream is never met with legitimacy, i.e., what if derby loses the personas and theatrics and yet is still not taken seriously by outsiders?

I pose these questions from the perspective that roller derby is a woman-centric sports organization embedded in a larger, masculine, patriarchal, and capitalist society. Though of course, I hope for derby's continued ability to empower its participants, I question derby's ability to maintain its emancipatory function as it pushes toward legitimacy. The sport may serve other important needs of its skaters, but it might lose its appeal as an empowering escape for the women who play. On the other hand, it is hard to fight for power and legitimacy while remaining a subordinated or disenfranchised population. I ended this section by posing questions as a way of imagining varying scenarios for how derby might develop and grow by within and against the power structures in which it is embedded.

Chapter 5 ended my foray into the world of derby by considering the overarching question of my study: *Why derby? Why now?* In this chapter, I analyzed the ways derby reflects larger trends in society, including the push for women to find empowering elements in their lives, whether athletic or otherwise. I argue that the rapid escalation of the sport's athleticism is a direct outgrowth of Title IX legislation. I also conceptualize roller derby as a gendered performance that provides women with an empowering outlet in which to experiment with various gender expressions. Finally, I looked to the future of derby by sharing the tension between mainstreaming to gain legitimacy or retaining original elements of derby, including its theatrics and personas.

While I embarked on a large qualitative study of roller derby by interviewing forty women, my study represents a mere snapshot in time. There is much to study within this large, expanding culture, both domestically and internationally. Future researchers could examine the reasons why women around the world play derby. I wonder whether skaters living in countries with more fluid gender expressions (i.e., less strict gender roles) play derby for similar or different reasons than do the American and Canadian women I interviewed. As junior derby and men's leagues are growing, future research could study the impact they have on the sport and culture of derby. In reality, roller derby as a site of study presents vast opportunities to contemplate the ways derby shapes and is shaped by society.

Conclusion

When first conceiving of this study years ago, and hearing how women use derby – whether with or without "true" alter egos – as an outlet to escape, I immediately thought of Virginia Wolf's *A Room of One's Own.* Virginia Woolf (1929) once wrote that women who want to write fiction need their own space, a "room of one's own," in order to be creative and successful. In this same vein, I wanted to understand how the "rink" empowers women with a setting to express themselves in ways not typically accepted in mainstream society. While this perspective was useful, as I delved further into data collection and analysis, I began to see that the women are drawn to the sport also because of the community aspect. In other words, I was thinking that they play derby *in spite of* the financial and time commitment as well as the promise of serious injury. However, I began to see that they played derby *because* of those three hurdles, or at least many of the women do. Although no one wants to suffer serious injury, especially if one's access to affordable health insurance is precarious, being connected to such a dangerous sport has an element of letting women demonstrate their physical toughness to others as well as themselves.

I also could not believe that, given how overworked and underpaid many Americans are, the women nevertheless commit to the sport, though it is akin to having a part-time job. Thus, I also began to see that perhaps *because* the women have so many demands in their life, derby functions as the perfect sport for them because it checks off a number of boxes simultaneously: exercise, physical contact/contact sport, an outlet for their aggression, and/ or exploring different aspects of the personality they feel on able to with her other parts of their life, the need for female friendships, and membership in an empowering, women-centric organization that gives back to the community. If you are going to have one "extra" in our busy lives, is there anything that provides so much depth and breadth to a woman's life as derby does?

References

Alvesson, M. & Billing, Y.D. (2009). *Understanding gender and organizations* (2nd ed.). Los Angeles, CA: Sage.

Arendt, C.E. & Buzzanell, P.M. (2017). Gender equality in the United States. In A. Örtenblad, R. Marling, & S. Vasiljević (Eds.), *Gender equality in a global perspective* (pp. 177–197). New York, NY: Routledge.

Berbary, L.A. & Johnson, C.W. (2016). En/activist drag: Kings reflect on queerness, queens, and questionable masculinities. *Leisure Sciences*, 1–14. DOI: 10.1080/01490400.2016.1194791

Brooke-Marciniak, B.A. & Varona, D.D. (2016, August 25). Amazing things happen when you give female athletes the same funding as men. Retrieved from www.

weforum.org/agenda/2016/08/sustaining-the-olympic-legacy-women-sports-and-public-policy/

Butler, J. (1990). Performative acts and gender constitution: An essay in pheno menology and feminist theory. In S. Case (Ed.), *Performing feminisms: Feminist critical theory and theatre*. Baltimore, MD: Johns Hopkins University Press.

Corbin, J. & Strauss, A. (2008). *Basics of qualitative research: Techniques and procedures for developing grounded theory* (3rd ed.). Thousand Oaks, CA: Sage.

Ely, R. & Padavic, I. (2007). A feminist analysis of organizational research on sex differences. *Academy of Management Review*, *32*, 1121–1143.

Grindstaff, L. & West, E. (2010). "Hands on hips, smiles on lips!" Gender, race, and the performance of spirit in cheerleading. *Text and Performance Quarterly*, *30*(2), 143–162.

Kotschwar, B. (2014). Women, sports, and development: Does it pay to let girls play? Retrieved from: https://piie.com/publications/pb/pb14-8.pdf

Levitt, H.M., Surace, F.I., Wheeler, E.E., Maki, E., Alcántara, D., Cadet, M., . . . Ngai, C. (2018). Drag gender: Experiences of gender for gay and queer men who perform drag. *Sex Roles*, *78*(5–6), 367–384.

Mumby, D., Thomas, R., Marti, I., & Seidl, D. (2017). Resistance redux. *Organization Studies*, *38*, 1157–1183.

National Coalition for Women and Girls in Education (NCWGE) (2012). Title IX and Athletics: Proved benefits and unfounded objections. Retrieved from: www. ncwge.org/TitleIX40/Athletics.pdf

National Coalition for Women and Girls in Education (NCWGE) (2017). Title IX at 45: Advancing opportunity through equity in education. Retrieved from: www. ncwge.org/TitleIX45/Title%20IX%20at%2045Advancing%20Opportunity%20 through%20Equity%20in%20Education.pdf

Olmstead, M. (2016, September 2). Title IX and the rise of female athletes in America. Retrieved from www.womenssportsfoundation.org/education/title-ix-and-the-rise – *of-female-athletes-in-america/*

Rubin, H.J. & Rubin, I.S. (2005). *Qualitative interviewing: The art of hearing data* (2nd ed.). Thousand Oaks, CA: Sage.

Rupp, L.J. & Taylor, V. (2003). *Drag queens at the 801 Caberet*. Chicago, IL: University of Chicago Press.

Rupp, L.J., Taylor, V., & Shapiro, E.I. (2010). Drag queens and drag kings: The difference gender makes. *Sexualities*, *13*(3), 275–294. DOI:10.1177/1363460709352725

Ryle, R. (2012). *Questioning gender: A sociological exploration*. Los Angeles, CA: Sage.

United States Department of Justice. (2015). Title IX of the education amendments Of 1972. Retrieved from www.justice.gov/crt/title-ix-education-amendments-1972

Vasiljević, S., Marling, R., & Örtenblad, A. (2017). Introduction: Different dimensions of gender equality in a comparative perspective. In A. Örtenblad, R. Marling, & S. Vasiljević (Eds.), *Gender equality in a global perspective* (pp. 3–19). New York, NY: Routledge.

West, C. & Zimmerman, D. (1987). Doing gender. *Gender & Society*, *1*, 125–151.

West, C. & Zimmerman, D.H. (2002). Doing gender. In S. Fenstermaker & C. West (Eds.), *Doing gender, doing difference: Inequality, power, and institutional change* (pp. 3–25). New York, NY: Routledge.

Wharton, A.S. (2012). *The sociology of gender: An introduction to theory and research* (2nd ed.).West Sussex, UK: Wiley – Blackwell.

Woolf, V. (1929). A room of one's own. Orlando, FL: Harcourt, Inc.

Appendix
Methodology

Paradigmatic rationale

I located my study within a critical-interpretive paradigm because the goals of my study best align with these two ontologies. First, I included the interpretive paradigm because I sought a "deeper" understanding of the lived experiences of the women who play roller derby from the women themselves (Corbin & Strauss, 2008; Rubin & Rubin, 2005). I utilize this perspective because, as an outsider who does not play derby, I needed to research and investigate as much as I could about this sport and community before I could add the layer of critique, which is what the critical perspective would provide.

Weaving critical theory with an interpretive perspective moves beyond gaining a deeper understanding by leaving open the possibility of criticizing "ideas and meanings expressed within social groups and situations being studied" (Alvesson & Billing, 2009, p. 43). As critical theorists aim to foreground the voices and interests of marginalized groups, a critical perspective emphasizes an inability to divorce a site of study from the power structures in which it is embedded. Specifically, I incorporated a critical lens because it calls on researchers to consider issues of power structures and inequalities, as well as moments of alienation or awareness and ultimately avenues of emancipation.

Methodological considerations

The key to any successful research study is choosing the appropriate methodology given the goals of the project. Because of my interest in gaining a deeper understanding of the power structures and inequalities and inequities within the derby community and the larger structures in which it is embedded, I chose a qualitative methodology. Lindlof and Taylor (2011) note that critical theorists have increasingly turned to qualitative methods "as a means of carefully describing everyday life" (p. 12).

Specifically, I utilized open-ended, semi-structured qualitative interviews to collect my data. I chose this method as it fits with my ontological and epistemological orientation as a researcher, specifically that participants should be given more freedom in and control of the research process (Creswell, 2007). Within the context of this study, qualitative interviewing generated a fairer or fuller representation of the interviewees' perspectives, which is especially relevant as this study seeks to connect participants' lived experiences with broader issues of power, gender, and emancipation.

Context and participants

The community of focus is women's roller derby within the United States and Canada. My research involved interviewing women who were currently playing roller derby. Upon obtaining Institutional Review Board (IRB) approval, I began recruiting women using the following requirements: (a) be active athletic participants (players) of roller derby, (b) be at least 18 years old, and (c) be located within the United States or Canada. If a woman was currently injured or pregnant, but still part of a league (i.e., intending to return to derby), I included her in my sample.

Participants. I began recruiting participants using the snowball method of sampling (Baxter & Babbie, 2004; Corbin & Strauss, 2008). A subset of purposive sampling, snowball sampling involves asking participants if they can suggest others who possess the same criteria or attributes through their social networks. This method is useful for difficult-to-reach populations or when discussing sensitive subjects (Berg, 2004).

I will later describe participants' demographics in aggregate in order to protect their identities. Because ethnic-racial identities are fluid, and more than 19 million people choose a catch-all category "some other race" by default on Census Data (U.S. Census Bureau, 2010), I chose to empower participants to express their ethnic-racial, gender, and sexual identities in their own terms. Of the forty women, thirty-four self-identified as White, while six women identified as the following: "Asian," "half-Asian," "Portuguese," "White/Asian/Native American," "Mexican/Aztec," or "Hispanic." The sample ranged in age from 22–45, with a mean age of 33.5. Fourteen women were in their twenties, fifteen were in their thirties, and nine of the women were in their forties. Regarding their relationship status, twenty women were single, thirteen were married, three were divorced, two were separated, and two were in a relationship. Ten of the women had children, and two women were pregnant at the time of the interview. The women varied in their educational backgrounds. When asked about their highest level of education, one woman said high school, one reported an Associate's Degree, five reported having "some college," nineteen women said a Bachelor's degree; two reported some Master's level coursework; seven have attained either a Master's of Arts or a Master's of Science; one had a Juris Doctor (J.D.), i.e., a law degree; two were currently enrolled in a Ph.D. program; and two women had doctorates (Ph.D.). Participants also varied in their professional backgrounds. Higher education was the most represented sector, with eight women who are either professors or working in other higher education positions, e.g., college counselor, financial aid, registrar. Some worked in the healthcare field as a nurse, EMT, athletic trainer, ER technician, or a physical therapist. Other women worked in law enforcement, politics, IT, journalists, data analysts, marketing, and advertising, and banking or finance. Three women were scientists, one woman was a civil engineer, one woman is an attorney, and another is a barista at a coffee shop. Three women reported being self-employed: one was a DJ, one was a small business owner, and one started her own healthcare consulting company.

My sample was dispersed geographically across the United States. The sample spanned twenty-three leagues across seventeen cities in both the United States (nineteen) and Canada (four) (some cities have multiple leagues and some women have played for more than one league). States represented in my sample include: Colorado, Connecticut, Illinois, Indiana, Maine, Minnesota, New York, Oklahoma, Oregon, Pennsylvania, Tennessee, and Wisconsin. With regard to their experience with roller derby, the women's time playing ranged from two months to eight years (and counting).

Perhaps most interesting about my sample is the range of experience and leadership roles taken throughout their leagues. I was lucky enough to interview a few women who brought roller derby to their state by founding a league, women who left one league to play in another league in the same city, women who have played internationally, women who have moved across the country not for work, but specifically for roller derby, and women who are a bit famous because of their talent as well as the team they play for. Other women have become coaches for the local men's leagues, and other women conduct outreach with junior derby and with women in other cities who want to start a league but who lack the knowledge of how to build a league. Finally, my sample included women playing on C level teams, which might be more for beginners, then B and A level teams, increasing in competitiveness, and also on all-star teams for their leagues. Some women came together to play in the World Cup, and relayed their fantastic experiences representing the United States.

Data collection

Interview procedures. After discussing my recruitment methods and participant demographics, I turn now to the data collection itself. First, I developed a semi-structured interview protocol (Smith, 1995). This means that I compiled and organized a list of general, open-ended questions and then each interview progressed differently as I listened to each answer and probed accordingly. My interview protocol was designed to explore five main foci: (a) how women became involved in roller derby, (b) how their participation was perceived and communicated in their close relationships, (c) how they described their roller derby persona, (d) how they articulated any benefits and consequences of the sport, and (e) how women perceived the future of the sport.

Questions aimed to explore how women became involved in roller derby, their role on committees, what level team they play on, what position they play, and any injuries they have had. To examine how their participation was perceived and communicated in their close relationships, I asked questions about what their family, friends, employers, and colleagues think about their participation. To better understand the ways in which players constructed personas, I asked questions regarding their derby persona: what their name is, how they chose it, whether they like playing under a persona or their own name, and the role, if any, the derby persona has played in their life, both within and outside of derby. The protocol also included questions about players' perceived benefits and consequences of the sport, as well as what they will take with them years after they have stopped playing. Last, questions geared to examine perceptions of the sport's future asked about their opinion on junior and men's leagues, and their visions and predictions for the sport; specifically whether they would like to see women's roller derby become an Olympic sport. I ended the interview by gathering any remaining demographic information I did not pick up throughout the course of the interview.

After assuring participants of confidentiality, I began by asking them if they have any questions for me. As an interviewer, I use the term confidentiality instead of anonymity, because confidentiality refers to the fact that I know their identity but promise to withhold that information from others. Anonymity, in contrast, is the proper term to use on anonymous surveys, where a researcher is unable to connect a participant's responses with his or her identity (Baxter & Babbie, 2004).

I conducted an initial four interviews before pausing data collection briefly (for one week) to reflect on the interviews and to examine what changes I needed to make, if any, to my interview protocol. I then proceeded to conduct the remaining thirty-six interviews using the amended protocol. This initial pause in my data collection follows a key principle of grounded theory, that researchers collect data and analyze it simultaneously from the initial phases of research (Charmaz, 2014).

With the interviewee's permission, I audio-recorded each interview, which I later had transcribed verbatim. While the transcripts did not include non-fluencies such as "um" or "uh," I tried to stay true to the participants' words by noting laughter, long pauses, word emphasis and requests for clarification. To indicate word emphasis, or an increase in volume, I capitalized entire words. I took notes as a backup, filling eight legal pads full of notes. I had another two legal pads of notes that I took and memos that I wrote throughout the process of data collection and analysis (Corbin & Strauss, 2008).

The forty interviews ranged from 27–160 minutes, with a mean length of 65 minutes, and resulted in 531 single-spaced transcribed pages. Upon transcribing the interviews, I gave each participant a pseudonym and removed their name from the transcript. In my ensuing write-ups, I made sure to mask any other identifying characteristic.

Data analysis

I drew upon principles of grounded theory throughout the data collection and analysis. According to the principles of grounded theory, grounded theory researchers collect data and analyze it simultaneously from the initial phases of research (Charmaz, 2014). As mentioned previously, I conducted an initial four interviews and then analyzed my notes and recordings for initial themes that helped guide the remaining thirty-six interviews. This approach combined two strategies of grounded theory: to collect and analyze data simultaneously and to pursue emergent themes through early data analysis. To identify emerging themes, I utilized open and axial coding. First, open coding involves identifying phenomena in the data and creating categories that represent the phenomena, while axial coding involves linking the grouping the numerous initial categories into subcategories. In other words, during open coding, you "fracture" data into separate pieces (categories), constructing distinct codes. Axial coding is the strategy for bringing the data back together (Charmaz, 2014, p. 147). The open coding resulted in more than a hundred initial codes. These codes were then combined with other codes or discarded as outliers. Each of the five chapters represents 10–15 of these codes that I coalesced into five thematic chapters. **Verification strategies.** Throughout the process of data collection and analysis, I was mindful of ensuring reliability and validity in this project. Therefore, I employed a series of strategies as suggested by Morse, Barrett, Mayan, Olson, and Spiers (2002). They suggest utilizing techniques such as sampling sufficiency, collecting and analyzing data concurrently, thinking theoretically, and developing theory. First, I analyzed the data while collecting it, a process appropriate to both the critical-interpretive ontology and the constant comparative method of grounded theory as it "forms a mutual interaction between what is known and what one needs to know" (Morse et al., 2002, p. 6). By considering what themes are emerging in the data while comparing it to previous knowledge from research and theories, I continuously considered how the data set contributes and extends theories. These strategies help ensure reliability and validity throughout critical-interpretive research.

I continued collecting and analyzing data until I reached a point of theoretical saturation, which occurs when "gathering fresh data no longer sparks new theoretical insights, nor reveals new properties of these core theoretical categories" (Charmaz, 2014, p. 213). I was pleased to reach theoretical saturation, given the geographical dispersion of my participants. Though participants were scattered across the United States and Canada, their experiences were very similar, in that what they considered negative consequences to playing, as well as the benefits they have gained from playing, were the same.

Limitations and future research

As with all research, the present study contains limitations. Though forty women participated in in-depth, open-ended interviews, I only employed one method of data collection. Future researchers could consider the value in large scale surveys or focus groups with derby athletes around the world. As I focused primarily on women currently participating, future research could expand parameters to include women who have retired, as well as anyone connected to the derby world such as coaches, referees, and even fans. Future research could also examine the growth of men's derby relative to the impact on women's derby, as well as the relationship between the male and female skaters.

Implications

This study examined the resurgence of women's roller derby across the United States and Canada, and the ways the sport fits into larger society.

A major finding of my study is that women need athletic outlets as well as venues that facilitate supportive, adult, female friendships. Despite living in a hypercompetitive, individualistic society that pressures people to place commitment to work and career over our social (and often familial) relationships, my data underscores the need for friendships and support networks. Additionally, data also suggest that participants need a place to experiment with their gendered expressions, and to rebel against gender norms. Though critical scholars find themselves concerned with issues of awareness and emancipation, true emancipation is hard to find, given numerous individual and societal constraints (namely overarching power structures). This study suggests that derby not only provides an awareness that is in itself empowering, but also serves an emancipatory function that is slowly, but undoubtedly, transforming what we know about women, sport, society, power, and gender.

References

Alvesson, M. & Billing, Y.D. (2009). *Understanding gender and organizations* (2nd ed.). Los Angeles, CA: Sage.

Baxter, L. A. & Babbie, E. (2004). *The basics of communication research*. Belmont, CA: Wadsworth.

Berg, B.L. (2004). *Qualitative research methods for the social sciences* (5th ed.). Boston: Pearson Publishing.

Charmaz, K. (2014). *Constructing grounded theory* (2nd ed). London: Sage.

Corbin, J. & Strauss, A. (2008). *Basics of qualitative research: Techniques and procedures for developing grounded theory* (3rd ed.). Thousand Oaks, CA: Sage.

Creswell, J.W. (2007). *Qualitative inquiry and research design: Choosing among five traditions* (3rd ed.). Thousand Oaks, CA: Sage.

Lindlof, T.R. & Taylor, B.C. (2011). *Qualitative communication research methods* (3rd ed). Thousand Oaks, CA: Sage.

Morse, J.M., Barrett, M., Mayan, M., Olson, K., & Spiers, J. (2002). Verification strategies for establishing reliability and validity in qualitative research. *International Journal of Qualitative Methods, 1*(2), 13–22.

Rubin, H.J. & Rubin, I.S. (2005). *Qualitative interviewing: The art of hearing data* (2nd ed.). Thousand Oaks, CA: Sage.

Smith, J.A. (1995). Semi-structured interviewing and qualitative analysis. In J.A. Smith, R. Harre, & L. Langenhove (Eds.), *Rethinking methods in psychology* (pp. 9–26). Thousand Oaks, CA: Sage.

U.S. Census Bureau. (2010). Intercensal estimates of the two or more races resident population by sex and age for the United States. Retrieved from: www.Census.gov/popest/data/intercensal/national/nat2010.html

Index